Mary and the Priestly Ministry

by

Fr. Emile Neubert, SM

T0204656

ACADEMY OF THE IMMACULATE
NEW BEDFORD, MA
2009

MARY AND THE PRIESTLY MINISTRY is a book prepared for publication by the Franciscans of the Immaculate [marymediatrix.com], POB 3003, New Bedford, MA 02741-3003.

Translated from the French:

MARIE ET NOTRE SACERDOCE

par E. NEUBERT, Marianiste

SPES - PARIS

1952

by Thomas A. Stanley, SM

Cum permissu superiorum

Fr. Stephanus M. Manelli, FI
Minister Generalis
February 11, 2009

The permission of the superiors is a declaration of the Roman Catholic Church that a work is free from error in matters of faith and morals, but in no way does it imply that she endorses the contents of the book.

ISBN: 978-1-60114-046-3

Mary and the Priestly Ministry

Fr. Emile Neubert, SM
Marianist

"for all my brother priests"

Contents

PART III

PERFORMING PRIESTLY MINISTRY WITH MARY

APPENDICES

Preface

The reader of this remarkable book is immediately plunged into the atmosphere of Lourdes. That, by itself, establishes its value and its merit.

At Lourdes, the Blessed Virgin Mary is a mediator and an educator, as every priest ought to be.

With her hands joined and her eyes lifted to heaven, this mediator offers to God our earthly pleas—those of Bernadette, who spontaneously falls to her knees and begins to pray, and those of the pilgrims, who continually do the same. As mediator, she receives only to give. Prayers rise up through her and graces descend through her. At Lourdes, graces flow as fully as do the waters of the river Gave.

As educator, the Virgin reaches out to the humble seer. By her appearance, her gestures, her words, and her smile, she fashions this soul into her own likeness.

The Virgin is also an educator for the pilgrims. Lourdes is the great school of the Christian faith. It is also a seminary. There, Mary manifests her mission to form the Church. A chapter of the history of Lourdes that may never be written is that of Mary's influence on the souls of priests—a very important part of its history.

With great pleasure, the Bishop of Tarbes and Lourdes expresses his gratitude to Father Emile Neubert for bringing priests into her school as their mother and their teacher. He earnestly recommends this outstanding book, *Mary and the Priestly Ministry*, to all his clerical brothers.

This publication answers a need and an expectation. Pressing contemporary exigencies indicate the necessity of the grace of closeness to Mary for success in the priestly ministry. Is this not the hour of Mary for priests as well as for the faithful?

It is clear to priests that the more deeply the influence of Our Lady penetrates their souls, the more priestly virtues and divine life they will have, and the more supernaturally fruitful their apostolic work for the glory of God will be.

Could we desire anything more? Is anything more urgent? This book—if meditated upon and lived out by many priests—will bring about a renewal of the Catholic priesthood.

+ Pierre Marie Theas

Bishop of Tarbes and Lourdes

PART I

LIVING CLOSE TO MARY—ITS
IMPORTANCE FOR A PRIEST

CHAPTER ONE

Discerning the Will of God

Before studying the doctrinal connections between Mary and the priestly ministry (which indicate the importance of living close to Mary), we must point out certain facts which manifest the will of God in this matter.

1. Our Holy Father, Pope Pius XII, "the Vicar of Christ," formally urges the priest to have a special devotion to Mary. In his apostolic exhortation, *Menti nostrae,* explaining the holiness of the sacerdotal life, addressed to all the priests of the world, he emphasizes this three times.

He says: "Inasmuch as priests can be called by a very special title, sons of the Virgin Mary, they will never cease to love her with an ardent piety, invoke her with perfect confidence, and frequently implore her strong protection."[1]

---

[1] *Menti nostrae,* n. 49.

Speaking of the spiritual formation to be given those seeking the priesthood, he declares: "And if, to devotion to the Blessed Sacrament, they unite filial devotion to the Most Blessed Virgin Mary, full of trust and abandonment to the Mother of God and urging the soul to imitate her virtues, then the Church will be supremely happy, because the fruit of an ardent and zealous ministry can never be wanting in a priest who, in adolescence, has been nurtured with the love of Jesus and Mary."[2]

Finally, before concluding his exhortation, the Holy Father emphasized once more the importance for priests to have absolute confidence in Mary's assistance, the remarkable success they will have when preaching devotion to Mary, and the special love Mary, the Mother of the Eternal Priest, has for all priests. The applicable quotation appears further on.

The priest who ignores the Pope lacks a truly Catholic spirit; his ministry will not be blest by God.

2. Ever since the role of Mary became better understood in the Church, all the great servants of the Gospel have been exceptionally devoted to the Blessed Virgin and have depended on her to

---

[2] Menti nostrae, n. 100.

achieve the marvels we admire in them: Bernard of Clairvaux, Francis of Assisi, Grignion de Montfort, Alphonse Liguori, Leonard of Port-Maurice, Abbe Poppe, Maximilian Kolbe, to name the more prominently known. To these can be added the names of priests currently distinguished for their powerful influence in diverse ministries. It is true that one can occasionally find priests who preach eloquently and attract a band of enthusiastic followers, but who give no evidence of an earnest and filial devotion to Mary. Sooner or later, their efforts prove to be shallow and short-lived, and sometimes even disastrous for their adherents and for themselves.

Thus, experience shows that devotion to Mary "succeeds" and that its absence leads to mediocrity and even to failure. And so, because all success comes from God, we must conclude that God wills this devotion and that we should embrace it even though we may not yet understand why he wills it. Understanding will come with practice.

3. It is at Lourdes, Saragossa, Fatima, Loreto, Beauraing, Banneux, and in similar sites in Germany, in Austria, in Switzerland, in Poland and in thousands of lesser known places throughout the world, that crowds of the faithful come to pray, to confess their sins, to receive the Eucharist, and to

reaffirm their faith and their Christian heritage. And those who do not have the opportunity to visit distant shrines, visit Mary in their cities and villages, actuating miracles of healing and especially of conversion wherever she is honored, transforming in less than twenty-four hours those whom the diocesan and religious clergy were unable to touch. The Catholic Faith has been maintained and strengthened in those places where personal effort on the part of the clergy has fostered the good will engendered by Mary, instead of calling it "just a passing fancy."

All this is a clear sign that it is the will of God that priests, "other Christs," seek the help of His Mother in carrying out their ministry.

4. This current age is the preeminent age of Mary. A great deal of evidence which will be elaborated further on makes this clear; one would have to be deliberately blind not to see it! The life of the Church is the life of Christ within the Church. Therefore, it is the will of God that He should hold the dominant place in all apostolic effort.

Furthermore, a multitude of signs indicate that it is the divine will that Mary should have a share in our priestly ministry. The supreme law for human beings is that they humbly and openly carry out the will of God. Any reasoning that contradicts this will has no value. "God wills it!" We have only to carry it out even though we do not understand the "why" of it.

There can be no success if the will of God is not carried out. The priest who has the zeal of St. Paul, the eloquence of St. John Chrysostom, the knowledge of St. Thomas, but who ignores the will of God, may perhaps be acclaimed and influence crowds, but he will not accomplish anything of supernatural value.

In the case at hand, does the will of God make any difficult demand of us? We are asked only to believe in His love for His Mother and for us, and to accept her involvement as the marvelous facilitator of our mission which makes us capable of saving and sanctifying ten or a hundred or a thousand times more souls.

CHAPTER TWO

Mother of Christ-Priest, and in a Special Way, Mother of Every Priest

In *Menti nostrae*, his exhortation to priests, Pius XII observed that "priests can be called by a very special title, sons of the Virgin Mary,"[3] and that she is "Mother of the Eternal Priest and therefore the loving Mother of all Catholic priests."[4] Let us take a closer look at the reasons for Mary's special mothering of priests.

The spiritual maternity of Mary, in regard to all the faithful, stems from her cooperation in the mysteries of the Incarnation, the Redemption, and the distribution of grace. Let us note how Mary, in these three functions, becomes Mother of priests in unique ways.

1. *The Incarnation Sets Special Grounds for Mary's Motherhood of Priests*

The Son of God became incarnate in order to be the Mediator between God and human beings, to be our High Priest. Every priest is taken from among men. Christ is not priest because He is Son of

---

[3] Menti nostrae, n. 49.

[4] Menti nostrae, n. 141.

God. How could He be mediator between Himself and humans? He is priest by reason of His human nature, hypostatically united to the Divinity.

Now Christ received His human nature from Mary. The Blessed Virgin, then, is involved in making the Son of God our Priest. He received His sacerdotal vocation from the Father. His sacerdotal anointing is the grace of the hypostatic union, gift of the Father, or more exactly, of the Holy Trinity. But it is His human nature, that enables the Son of God to be Priest, and it was Mary who gave it to Him.

To put it in terms of scholastic theology, Mary provided the material cause of Christ's priesthood. But she did not do so blindly. She knew that the Messiah, whose mother she would be, was to be a priest according to a new and eternal priesthood. *Tu es sacerdos in aeternum secundum ordinem Melchisedech* (Ps 109:4). She knew that the priesthood of the Son of God was contingent upon her response. She was then a fully cognizant, free, and responsible cause of Christ's priesthood. Mary is the Mother of our God, Mother of our Creator, Mother of our Lawgiver, Mother of our Rewarder. Had she responded negatively to the message of the angel, the Son of God would still be God, Creator,

Lawgiver and Rewarder, but He would not be Priest
and no Christian would become a priest.

In the mystery of the Incarnation, Mary becomes
the Mother of all the faithful, because in giving life
to our Head, she simultaneously gives it to all the
members of the Mystical Body of Christ. This is
how Pope Pius X explains the spiritual maternity of
Mary in view of her cooperation in the mystery of
the Incarnation:

"Isn't Mary the Mother of God?" the Pope asks.
And by that fact he determines, "She is also our
Mother."

> Indeed everyone must believe that Jesus,
> the Word made Flesh, is also the Savior of
> the human race. Now, as the God-Man He
> acquired a body composed like that of other
> men, but as Savior of our race He had a kind
> of spiritual and mystical body, which is the
> society of those who believe in Christ. *We,
> the many, are one body in Christ* (Rom 12:5),
> but the Virgin conceived the Eternal Son not
> only that He might be made man by taking
> His human nature from her, but also that by
> means of the nature assumed from her He
> might be the Savior of men. For this reason
> the angel said to the shepherds, *Today in the*

*town of David a Savior has been born to you,
who is Christ the Lord* (Lk 2:11). So in one and
the same bosom of His most chaste Mother,
Christ took to Himself human flesh and at
the same time united to Himself the spiritual
body built up of those *who are to believe in
Him* (Jn 17:20).

Consequently Mary, bearing in her womb
the Savior, may be said to have borne also all
those whose life was contained in the life of
the Savior. All of us, therefore, who are united
with Christ and are, as the Apostle says,
*members of His body, made from His flesh and
from His bones* (Eph 5:30), have come forth
from the womb of Mary as a body united to
its head. Hence, in a spiritual and mystical
sense, we are called children of Mary, and
she is the Mother of us all: 'The Mother in
spirit…but truly the Mother of the members
of Christ, which we are.'[5]

Saint Paul tells us that the members of the
Mystical Body of Christ do not have the same role,
but that each one has a unique function. The special
role of the priest in this Body is to extend His
priesthood. Mary then carried all her Son's future

---

[5] Pope St. Pius X, *Ad diem illum*.

priests in her womb along with Him. She did not know them individually at that time, but she wished for them what Jesus wished for them at that time, and loved them with the same special love her Son had for them.

All this gives us some idea of the special ties that exist between Mary and priests. It helps us to take into account how much the priestly ministry involves the Mother of Christ, the High Priest, and how indispensable that involvement is.

2. *Our Mother Mary's Special Role in the Redemption*

If Mary, in the Incarnation, conceived us spiritually, as it were, then in the mystery of the Redemption she gave us birth. It was then, in subservience to the action of her Son that she brought about our freedom from the death of sin and the bestowal of the grace of divine life.

There, the sufferings and self-sacrifice she underwent on our behalf were offered, as were those of her Son, for the whole human race. But in the same way that her Son, in shedding His Blood for all (and not separate drops for special souls), had the intention of benefiting certain souls more than others (His Mother, first of all, then the apostles and their successors, and chosen individuals through the ages), so Mary also had the intention of helping certain individuals more than others through her sufferings. Among them, were certainly those men who would commit themselves to the work of her Son—the priests.

There is a widespread tendency to offer, as proof of the spiritual maternity of Mary, the words spoken to her by the dying Christ: *Behold your Son* (Jn 19:26). No doubt, the immediate intention of Jesus was to confide to the care of the beloved disciple His mother, a widow since the death of Joseph, for she would remain on earth after He was gone. But He certainly had in mind a deeper and broader message regarding Mary's spiritual maternity to all the faithful.[6] These words did not create that maternity, for then it would be merely an adoptive, superficial maternity, and not a real, innate one. As we have seen, it was the cooperation of Mary in the mysteries that brought about our supernatural life (the Incarnation and the Redemption) that constitute the basis of this maternity. These words of Christ are meant to confirm her spiritual maternity, and they proclaim the culmination of it, at the very moment the mystery of the Redemption itself is achieved.

---

6 Cf. Marie dans le dogme (E. Neubert) pp. 76–79.

Note that at the foot of the Cross, there were other persons seemingly more likely to be chosen by Christ to care for His Mother. There was that other Mary, wife of Clopas, the brother of St. Joseph, and mother of James, who, in a few days, would be favored with a special appearance of the risen Christ and who would eventually be the first bishop of Jerusalem. There was Mary Magdalen, sister of Martha and Lazarus. We know the affection Christ had for this family and for Magdalen in particular; and so this former sinner, now become the favored daughter of Mary, Refuge of Sinners, would be a fitting choice. At the same time, we should also note that John's mother, Salome, was still alive, so he didn't seem to need a second mother.

Nonetheless, it was to John that Christ confided Mary. That is because John was a priest and it is to priests, above all, that Christ gives His Mother because He has a greater love for them and they have a greater need of her. John writes in his Gospel, *And from that hour the disciple took her into his own home* (Jn 19:27). Would that all priests would appreciate the implication of this and, like John, take Mary into their lives.

3. *Our Mother Mary's special role in the distribution of grace*

The death of Christ *merited* for us the supernatural life of grace *primordially* but it was not immediately conferred on us. It had yet to be conferred on each of us individually in the form of sanctifying grace and actual graces. It is Mary, disseminator of all graces, who obtains them for us. They are bestowed on everyone, but not in the same measure. Some individuals receive much more than others.

In this matter, priests hold a place apart. Who can list all the special graces she procures for them? Generally they are born into, and raised within, a very Catholic family. They receive calls to greater purity, holiness, and generosity at relevant moments. They become aware of an invitation to a more significant life, sometimes extended often and over a long period of time, and accompanied by the graces of strength and enlightenment needed to overcome hesitations and obstacles. Countless graces are bestowed on them during the time of preparation for the priesthood, especially the graces conferred at the reception of the various Sacred Orders, that of the priesthood most of all. And how many additional graces since receiving the power to offer up the Divine Victim! These include the opportunity for daily Mass; more immediate contact with the supernatural in the exercise of the ministry;

compelling requests to give of oneself completely and come to the help of many individuals in distress; feelings of accountability, remorse, regret, and encouragement when encountering special souls who exhibit a delicate conscience; and limitless generosity. The Blessed Mother never ceases to flood them with graces to the extent that they are capable of receiving them. She would be happy to bestow a hundred times more, if only greater confidence in her and greater union with her would enlarge their hearts, permitting her to bring them this increase.

4. *Our Mother Mary's Special Love for Priests*

If maternity consists essentially in giving and in nurturing life, can any human maternity be understood apart from such a love? Must it not be so understood in the most perfect of mothers above all? Mary loves all the faithful with an incomparable love. But she loves priests with an altogether unique love, and that, for a number of reasons.

a) She sees in the priest a greater resemblance to the image of her Son than in any other Christian of equal holiness. Jesus became incarnate primordially for the glory of God and the salvation of souls. The laity participates in the priesthood of Christ in a wide sense, but they are not priests in the strict sense of the word. They face many difficulties in their efforts to work directly for the glory of God and the salvation of the world.

The priest, on the other hand, fits more closely the definition of Christ-Priest; he is another son-of-God-become-man for the glory of God and the salvation of souls.

b) Jesus loves His priests with a distinctive love. It suffices to read the discourse He gave at the Last Supper to grasp the tenderness that He showed for His new priests. *No longer do I call you servants, for the servant does not know what his master is doing; but I have called you friends, for all that I have heard from my Father I have made known to you. You did not choose me, but I chose you and appointed you that you should go and bear fruit and that your fruit should abide; so that whatever you ask the Father in my name, he may give it to you* (Jn 15:15–16). It is these compassionate words of Christ that the bishop, in Jesus' name, addresses to priests at the time of their ordination.

Mary shares all the feelings of her Son. Those who are particularly cherished by Jesus are particularly cherished by her.

c) It is thanks to priests, above all, that the work of Christ is carried out in the world. Without their collaboration (unhappy experiences prove it all too well), the Christian religion flounders; Jesus has shed His Blood in vain.

How can Mary, who has no other interests than those of Jesus, fail to have a special love for those committed to give a worldwide efficacy to the mission of her Son, for those destined to make efficacious in souls the Blood He shed for them?

d) In her union with her Son, Jesus, Priest and Victim, she foresaw especially those who would continue her Son's mission on earth. For them, above all, as we have already pointed out, she offered prayers and sufferings and the very life of her Son. And ever since, how ceaselessly she prays to the Father for their sanctification and their success! The more one prays and suffers for someone, the more one loves that person. How much love must she not have for those for whom she has prayed and suffered so much?

e) She needs priests. It is especially through them that she can carry out her mission of giving Jesus to the world, of sanctifying souls and transforming them into other Christs. Without them, all these beloved souls for whom she has prayed and suffered and offered her Son, are in danger of being eternally separated from their Mother, of being eternally lost! But priests can assist her in leading them to the Father and to their Mother, and in achieving happiness for all eternity. How much grateful love must she have for them?

All these reasons help us better understand the concluding words of Pope Pius XII's apostolic exhortation regarding the sanctity of the sacerdotal life: "Our Lady loves everyone with a most tender love, but she has a particular predilection for priests who are the living image of Jesus Christ. Take comfort in the thought of the love of the divine Mother for each of you and you will find the labors of your sanctification and priestly ministry much easier... To the Beloved Mother of God, Mediatrix of heavenly graces, We entrust the priests of the whole world in order that, through her intercession, God will vouchsafe a generous outpouring of his spirit which will move all ministers of the altar to holiness and, through their ministry, will spiritually renew the face of the earth."[7]

---

[7] *Menti nostrae*, n. 142–143.

CHAPTER THREE

Mary, Associate of Christ-Priest, Whose Vicars are the Priests

Mary is not only the Mother of Christ-Priest, and in consequence, Mother of all priests, she is also His Associate in His priesthood.

It is historically evident that in the understanding of the Christian faithful, Mary participates in all the prerogatives and all the operations of Christ's humanity in the manner and to the extent that her status, as creature and woman, allows for her participation in the eminence of an Incarnate God.[8] She is, according to the rich expression of St. Albert the Great, the *socia Christi* (Associate of Christ), and she is such in regard to the Redemption, the distribution of graces, the Kingship of Christ, and His priesthood as well.

Consequently, it is in the light of Christ's priesthood that Mary's role here should be studied, and not in the light of the sacerdotal ministry of priests.

---

8 Cf. De la decouverte progressive des grandeurs de Marie (E. Neubert) Spes 1951, Chap. 3 "Le point de vue du peuple fidele" pp. 43–62 (especially p. 56).

When identifying the elements that make up the priesthood, we find the following in the Epistle to the Hebrews: The priest is taken from among men—by a special calling—consecrated or anointed—as mediator—between a God to be appeased—and human creatures needing to be reconciled to him—by the offering of a sacrifice.

Several of these elements are found in all the faithful. All of them (with the exception of the last one) are present in lay religious, especially those who are contemplatives. These individuals are taken from among the faithful, called by a God-given vocation, consecrated by their religious profession to be mediators between God (to whom they offer their expiatory sacrifices) and all men and women (for whom they petition pardon and needed graces). And yet they do not exercise the priesthood, properly understood, because they are not enabled to offer the sacrifice of the New Law. It is the power to offer this particular Sacrifice that constitutes the identifying characteristic of the Catholic priest.

Here, sacrifice is understood as every total offering made to God to recognize his complete dominion. In this sense, everyone can offer sacrifices to God. *Through him (Christ) then let us continually offer up a sacrifice of praise to God, that is, the fruit of lips that acknowledge his name. Do not neglect to do good and to share what you have, for such sacrifices are pleasing to God* (Heb 13:15–16).

A sacrifice can consist of something wholly internal. *Were I to give a burnt offering, you would not be pleased. The sacrifice acceptable to God is a broken spirit* (Ps 51:16–17). It can also consist of something both internal and external, the external element signifying the internal disposition.[9]

In the sacrifices offered to God in the name of the people by someone designated to represent them as mediator before God, i.e., as a priest, both elements are present. This is an apt reflection of human nature[10] and needed to allow for the participation of the people. If the internal element is lacking, God rejects the offering. According to the prophets, this was often the case in Old Testament times.

During New Testament times, God no longer desires ancient-type sacrifices; now, the only Sacrifice is that of Christ. *When Christ came into the world, he said, 'Sacrifices and offerings thou hast not desired, but a body hast thou prepared for me; in burnt offerings and sin offerings thou hast taken no pleasure.' Then I said, 'Lo I have come to do thy will, O God,'… and by that will we have been sanctified through the*

---

9 Aquinas, Summa Theologica, II, 11, q. 85, a. 1.
10 Ibid.

offering of the body of Jesus Christ once for all (Heb 10:5–7, 10).

Let us now apply these observations to the priesthood of Christ and to the position of Mary cooperating in His sacrifice.

As the Incarnate God, Christ is the Priest— our needed Mediator—called to this office by the Most Holy Trinity—consecrated by the grace of the hypostatic union—to propitiate God offended by humankind—bringing pardon to all men and women, along with the grace of adoption—and this, by sacrificing Himself on the Cross.

He did not immolate Himself by His own hands, it is true, but He voluntarily abandoned Himself to the hands of His executioners who were the unknowing ministers of His sacerdotal immolation. *Oblatus est quia ipse voluit [He was immolated because He Himself willed it]* (Is 53:7, Vulgate text). It is this immolation (the material element) lovingly willed (the spiritual element), which constitutes the priestly action.

The Blessed Virgin was taken from among the human race—predestined from all eternity to be associated with Christ in the work of our redemption—consecrated for this endeavor by the grace of the divine Maternity—Mediatrix of all grace beside the Mediator of justice—contributing with Him and in dependence on Him in propitiating God—and in winning graces for all men and women—and that 1) by the union of her will and sufferings with the will and sufferings of her Son (the spiritual element); and 2) by the forsaking of her maternal rights in regard to Jesus' immolation (the material element).

This "material element" requires some explanation. Popes Benedict XV and Pius XII expressly mention Mary's forsaking of her maternal rights regarding Jesus as an element of her status as Coredemptrix. What are these maternal rights?

It is not a question of legal right—Jesus was an adult. But in addition to formal, legal rights, there are *natural rights* which adulthood does not obliterate.

In his very nature a son carries something of his mother. He receives his body and his very life from her. The nurturing she gives him reflects all that is the best, the noblest, and the most generous in her. She exemplifies for him a love most tender, ever constant, completely selfless, and often heroic. And all these benefactions make him an extension and a part of her with the consequence that whatever pleases him, pleases her; whatever he suffers, she suffers; and when he dies, something more precious than her own life dies in her.

These, then, are Mary's maternal rights regarding her Son. But in Mary's case, these rights were more intense than in any other mother. A woman who becomes a mother has meaning independently of her motherhood. She could renounce marriage and still achieve her mission as a human being. If she becomes a mother, she is such for all her children and not for just one of them, and she shares her parenthood with a father. Mary's motherhood, however, was uniquely for her only Son. She existed only for Him and she alone formed Him. Conversely, He took everything from her, who, in the words of de Berulle, was "pure capacity for Jesus." Take Jesus from her, and you take away her reason for existing—you take away her very life!

It is true that it is God who owns all rights regarding the humanity of Christ. Strictly speaking, a creature cannot claim any rights that belong to the Creator. But in working with free human beings, God shows almost infinite deference; he almost treats them as equals. He respects the gifts he has given to his creatures. In giving her his Son, he first asked the Blessed Virgin for her consent; in taking Him from her, he again sought her agreement.

It is true that in the Old Law, anyone supplying a victim to a priest and uniting himself to the intentions and will of the one carrying out the sacrifice, does not, by that fact, become a co-priest. That is because he has not received a sacerdotal vocation or anointing. But we must not forget that Mary, by her gift of the divine Maternity, was called to be for Christ an *adjutorium simile sibi* (a helper like Himself), to be simultaneously *mater et socia Christi* (Mother and Associate of Christ).

But was the abandonment of her maternal rights regarding Jesus a self-immolation? Yes, in the same way that Christ's abandonment of His Body to His executioners was a self-immolation. *Oblatus est quia ipse voluit*. (He was immolated because He Himself willed it). The same can be said of His Auxiliary: *Oblatus est quia ipsa voluit (She was immolated because she herself willed it).*

The cooperation of Mary in the priesthood of Christ is similar to her cooperation in the redemptive mission of Christ. These two functions are correlative. Christ redeemed us by His Sacrifice, and to offer a sacrifice, He had to be a priest. The priestly sacrifice is the cause; redemption is the effect.

It was the determination of God that this Sacrifice should be necessary for our redemption. Other actions performed by Christ after His birth were, in themselves, sufficient to redeem us, but, in fact, were simply oriented toward this Sacrifice.

Mary is the perfect Associate of Christ in the offering of this redemptive sacrifice through a material element (giving in to the death of her Son), and by a spiritual element (a complete union of her will and her sacrifices to those of Christ). Her cooperation, then, was eminently sacerdotal.

The association of Mary with Christ as Redeemer and as Priest presents a parallel that allows us to determine, in a rather precise fashion, the nature of Mary's sacerdotal cooperation in the Sacrifice on Cavalry, given the recent studies of her role as Coredemptrix.

The role of the Coredemptrix in our redemption is not identical with that of the Redeemer, but merely analogous to it. It is not hers by necessity but only by the loving will of God. It is a secondary one—not a principal one. It is dependent on that of Jesus and not self-sufficient. It is carried out in union with the action of her Son and not apart from it. In fact, the sacerdotal action of Mary, carried out as Coredemptrix, is only present by the will of

God. It is secondary and dependent on the action of Jesus, to which it is united in its performance and its effects. Together, Jesus and Mary offer the same redemptive sacrifice, He as the Second Adam and she as the *adjutorium simile sibi* (the helper like Himself).

What term should be used to describe the role of the Blessed Virgin in this Sacrifice? Several have been suggested, but they are ambiguous and only confuse the issue. It seems that the most coherent one is that of Saint Albert the Great: *Associate of Christ the High Priest* (*socia Christi sacerdotis*). The phrase *socia Christi* (Associate of Christ) has a precise meaning in Marian theology. It signifies a secondary action—analogous to and united with that of Christ—the action of a helper akin to Him.

These understandings have to do with the material element of the Sacrifice of the Cross, the immolation of the Victim. With regard to the spiritual element, i.e., the union of the prayers, sufferings, and will of Mary with the prayers, sufferings, and will of Christ the High Priest in view of the expiation offered to God and the gaining of grace for humankind, they are of the same duration and proportionally of the same intensity in Mary as in Jesus. In her, as in Him, they are carried out to the extreme limit of their power to love and to suffer. Like Jesus, Mary willed this Sacrifice from that moment when, by becoming the Mother of God, she offered herself as His Associate in the work of Redemption. From the moment she replied to Gabriel: *Ecce ancilla Domini; fiat mihi secundum verbum tuum [Behold, I am the handmaid of the Lord; let it be to me according to your word]* (Lk 1:38), the Word become flesh in her womb said to His Father: *Ecce venio…ut faciam voluntatem tuam [Lo, I have come to do thy will]* (Heb 10:7).

She consented to furnish the Victim composed of her own substance. She acquiesced with full knowledge of this because she knew from Isaiah, the destiny which awaited her Son. Simeon clearly reminded her of this at the moment he announced the sorrowful role she would have in the Sacrifice.

She nurtured the Victim in view of this Sacrifice. As Jesus grew in age, the closer the fatal hour came. Her *fiat* became ever more sorrowful and yet, ever more determined and loving. She renewed it repeatedly, especially at the time of the Passion, at each step of this terrible martyrdom. It was then, above all, that she united herself to the will of the Father regarding her Son, and to the intentions of her Son regarding the Father and the redemption of humankind. Her will, her love, and her sufferings were entirely one with those of her Son. She offered Him, and offered herself with Him.

Such is the participation of the Blessed Mother in the priesthood of Christ. On occasion, the title Virgin-Priest has been given her. It is possible to give this title an orthodox interpretation, but it is ambiguous and frowned upon by Rome. Those who use it wish, thereby, to enhance the grandeur of Mary. In reality, however, it carries the risk of reducing the role of the Associate of Christ-Priest to that of a simple minister. Mary played a real part in the Sacrifice of the Cross—a part of unlimited suffering and love that lasted thirty-three years. In the Sacrifice of the Mass, the minister merely lends his hands and his voice to Jesus, but it is Jesus who is the actual Priest.

According to the teaching of Saint Pius X, Mary, "as associate with Christ in the work of human salvation, merited for us *de congruo (fittingly)*, as the expression has it, what Christ merited for us *de condigno (rightfully)*." The priest merits nothing during the sacramental enactment of the mystery of our Redemption; he merely brings into play a part of the graces merited by Christ *de condigno* and by Mary *de congruo*.

At her place beside the immolated Lamb, Mary remains His Associate throughout eternity, in His immolation. The priest must repeat the Sacrifice each day and this Sacrifice will cease at the end of the world.

When God calls an individual to a special mission, he gives that person the graces needed to carry out the mission. Accordingly, he gives priests the special graces they need, but to Mary he has given incomparably more graces than to all priests together.

Furthermore, according to the thought of Saint Albert the Great, Mary transcends all the faithful, even the most elevated members of the ecclesiastical hierarchy, not only by her divine Maternity, but also by her place beside Christ the High Priest. He states: "Every religious congregation in the Church has a ministry. But the Blessed Virgin Mary was not chosen by God for a ministry but in view of an association and as an assistant (*in consortium et adjutorium*). In the words of Scripture, 'I will make him a helper fit for him.' The Blessed Virgin is not a surrogate; she is an aid and companion (*Beata Virgo non est vicaria sed coadjutrix et socia*)."[11]

---

[11] Mariale, q. 42, t. 38, 81, AB. In 1954 the Mariale was proven to be a spurious work of St. Albert the Great. The actual author (now referred to as Pseudo-Albert)

If, from all eternity, this is the place the Most Holy Trinity wished to assign the Blessed Virgin in predestining her to be *Mater et socia Christi,* and particularly if the divine Word wished to involve her with His priesthood so intimately, and at the cost of so much sorrow to her and to Himself, how can priests not follow as completely as possible, the eternal plan of God and the desire of our High Priest and, in like manner, grant the Blessed Virgin a similar involvement in their priesthood? Jesus wished to make all priests His intimate friends. Friendship means a sharing of purpose and feeling. The exhortation of Saint Paul: *Sentite in vobis quod in Christo Jesu [Have this mind among yourselves which is in Christ Jesus]* (Phil 2:5), applies especially to priests. They should make the Blessed Virgin an associate in their priesthood as He did. It is only in this way that their priesthood will fully resemble that of Christ, a way that was foreseen and decreed from all eternity and actualized on Calvary.

---

and time of writing are unknown. Fr. Neubert was unaware of this at the time he wrote (1952). Yet there are many valuable and valid insights in this work, the most important of which is that of Mary as socia (Associate) of Christ. Many insights and phrases in it continue to be cited.

CHAPTER FOUR

Mary, Symbol and Mother of the Church, Whose Agents are the Priests

Mary-Church has been a cherished parallel for Christians from early times. For them, the Church has been, like Mary, a mother, a spouse, and a virgin. This parallel is encountered frequently up to the eighteenth century. In recent years, it has resurfaced and been probed more than ever. Important historical studies have examined it in the traditions of patrology and theology. Dogmatic theses have explored it with promising and interesting results.[12]

There is more than a simple parallel between Mary and the Church. With Christ, Mary gave birth to the Church on Calvary. At its start, she was the Church. And the Church which began with her continues on earth the functions Mary carries out in heaven—she gives birth to the faithful, nourishes and nurtures them, leading them to the full stature of Christ.

As a consequence, all priests, as representatives of the Church, should maintain a particularly close

---

[12] Cf. les Bulletins de la Societe Francaise d'Etudes mariales de 1951, 52, 53. Lethielleux Edit.

relationship with Mary. Properly speaking, it is through their efforts that the Church gives birth to, nourishes and nurtures the faithful, helping them to become other Christs. Intimate union with Mary will enable them to do this best of all, to serve the Church the best way possible.

CHAPTER FIVE

Similarities and Parallels between Mary and the Priest

Even though the role of Associate of Christ-Priest is different than that of the sacerdotal minister of the Holy Sacrifice of the Mass and surpasses it beyond measure, there are, nevertheless, remarkable similarities and parallels between Mary and the priest. Their respective functions both have to do with the Sacrifice of the Cross. Let us point out the principal ones.

According to a generally held opinion, Mary, from the first moment she knew her Creator and because of her Immaculate Conception, gave herself completely to him for whatever he should ask of her. In the same way, most priests received an early-in-life invitation to give themselves to God.

That she might belong irrevocably to God, Mary consecrated herself to Him at an early age by a vow of virginity. Before his definitive commitment of God in the priesthood, the seminarian makes a solemn commitment to celibate chastity.

The Blessed Virgin received her vocation explicitly from God by the words of an angel. Properly speaking, the seminarian receives his vocation from God through the bishop who admits him to Orders.

It is by the grace of the divine Maternity that Mary becomes the Associate of Christ-Priest. It is by the grace of ordination that a deacon becomes a priest.

The divine Maternity engages Mary in a permanent and eternal relationship with Christ-Priest. Ordination to the priesthood marks the soul of a priest with an ineffaceable and eternal character that includes a special relationship to Christ-Priest.

Mary gave substantial existence to Christ-Priest when she gave Him a physical body. The priest gives

Him a new, accidental existence in giving Him a Eucharistic body.

Mary offers up the Holy Victim in union with Jesus. The priest offers Him up in repeating the words of Jesus. Mary offers up the divine Victim with Jesus to accede to the will of God and to obtain grace for humankind. The priest offers up the same Victim for the same purposes and on behalf of particular individuals.

Mary is the Coredemptrix at the Sacrifice of the Cross. The priest is a co-redeemer within the Sacrifice of the Mass and in mediating the effects of the Redemption.

Mary is the Distributrix of all the graces of the Redemption. The priest is a disseminator in subordination to Mary of some of these gifts.

Everything Mary does is an effort to give Jesus to the world. Similarly, the mission of the priest is to bring Jesus to the world.

Mary's participation in the mysteries of the Incarnation and the Redemption makes her the spiritual mother of souls. In a parallel way the priest has a spiritual paternity with regard to the souls confided to him. In fact, one could almost say a *maternity* since he acts in the name of two mothers—Mary and the Church.

In order to carry out her mission in regard to Jesus and contribute to the glory of God and the salvation of humankind, Mary was predestined to a holiness without equal. Called to perform actions similar to those of the Blessed Virgin, the priest should strive for the holiness to which his special graces call him.

Mary existed only for God and, from the time of the divine Maternity, only for Jesus and for souls. From the time of his ordination, a priest no longer exists for himself; he must live for Christ and with Christ, for the Father and for souls.

The life of the Associate of Christ-Priest was a life of prayer and unimaginable suffering. The priest must be a man of prayer and accept hardships beyond those of other men.

The parallel can be continued to show how the qualities and dispositions of Christ-Priest were those of His Associate and ought to be those of every priest. This idea will be developed at length in the second part of this book.

Concerning the dignity of all these functions, those of Mary are the most eminent, surpassing those of all other creatures to an immeasurable degree. Next to hers are those of the priest, exceeding even those of the angels.

When individuals share the same task, the same goals and dispositions, the same outlook and convictions, the same joys and sorrows, they tend by nature to form a close companionship. And the more authentic their motives, the more disinterested their actions, the more noble their goal and the more passionate their desire to attain it, the closer and stronger is their fellowship. Then how much more intimate and special should be the union between the priest and the Mother and Associate of Christ High Priest?

CHAPTER SIX

The Priest Has a Fundamental Need of Mary

We have seen that Mary needs the priest. But the priest needs Mary even more. Mary mediates many graces, even the majority of them, without the help of a priest. But the priest cannot procure any grace for any creature without the intervention of Mary.

We know from the teaching of the Church and from tradition that every heavenly gift comes to us through Mary, the Mediatrix of all graces.

Priests themselves would not be priests if Mary had not obtained for them the grace of their vocation as well as all the graces that led them to the priesthood.

Priests exercise their ministry successfully, but this ministry would be sterile without God's grace, i.e., without a special intervention of Mary.

Every conversion of a sinner that they bring about needs the help of grace; it is with Mary's help that this occurs. Every soul that they lead from apathy to fervor, they bring about with the help of grace and, therefore, with the help of Mary. If their teaching, or their preaching, or their ability to organize brings about redemptive results, it is with the help of grace, and so it is Mary who mediates these wonders. Do away with the sun, and the earth no longer has light, warmth, or life. Do away with the intervention of Mary, and souls no longer have life, or warmth, or life. Priestly ministry becomes powerless.

Mary, it is true, obtains these graces even for those who do not pray to her for them. But it goes without saying that she obtains immensely more for those who invoke her name. And what a difference there is between Christians who ignore her and those who are her avid adherents. And this does not come about only because Mary naturally favors her generous and loving children over those who ignore their Mother, but also and especially because it is the will of God. If he has decided that no grace shall be given to a human being except through her, he will mitigate his graces for those who ignore his will. In contrast he will lavish them on those who, in accordance with his loving plan, ask favors of him through her.

What is true for the faithful in general, is all the more so for priests. These chosen and consecrated ones, these *other Christs,* should be more aware than other Christians of God's loving plan for His Mother. How can he bless their work if they do not carry out their filial responsibilities?

Why has such an extraordinary privilege been accorded to Mary? It is not by way of an arbitrary decision made by Jesus out of love for His Mother. It is in consequence of her role as Coredemptrix and her involvement in His priestly function. All graces, without exception, have been merited by the Passion.

As Associate in the Passion of Her Son, Mary made a contribution to the winning of these graces. Is it not natural then, that she should be involved in the distribution of these graces? "She shared the labor; she should also share the honor." Moreover, the Popes who explain the union of Mary with her Son in our redemption, see her role as Distributrix of all graces as a consequence of her union with the suffering Christ, High Priest.

Leo XIII teaches this doctrine in several encyclicals. In the encyclical, *Adjutricem populi*, for example, he writes: "From the time (of her Assumption) Mary, by a divine decree, watches over the Church, assists and protects it as a mother. For, having been a collaborator in the mystery of the Redemption, she became a similar collaborator in regard to the graces which flow forever from this mystery, giving her unlimited power, as it were, in this matter." Note how the Sovereign Pontiff ties the distribution of grace to its acquisition in the Redemption.

There is a like statement and explanation by St. Pius X. In his encyclical, *Ad diem illum,* he says: "Because of the union of suffering and intent between Mary and Christ, she rightfully merits becoming the Reparatrix of a sinful world, and in consequence of that, the Dispensatrix of all the gifts Jesus acquired for us by His suffering and death."

Benedict XV expresses the same thought and gives the same explanation. "Because of the Blessed Virgin's involvement in the redemptive Passion," he writes, "graces of every sort that we receive from the treasury of the Redemption are all received, so to say, from the hands of the Sorrowful Mother."[13]

Now, if it is only by grace that something supernatural can occur, and if it is only through Mary that graces are given to humans, it follows that no priest can successfully exercise his ministry except with her. And the more closely a priest is united to the Distributrix of all graces, the more profound, the more comprehensive, and the more wondrous his work with souls will be. Does this not explain the statements made in Chapter One?

---

13 *Acta Apostolicae Sedis*, X, 182.

PART II

MARY FORMS THE PRIEST AS ANOTHER CHRIST-PRIEST

NOTE: *Much has been written since Saint John Chrysostom concerning the obligations and sanctity of the priestly life. Since the beginning of the 20th century this subject has been explored with increasing interest. Popes Pius X, Pius XI, and Pius XII in particular, have addressed to the clergy teachings and directives appropriate for modern times. Workaday priests (and this fact is most encouraging) are becoming more and more aware of their responsibilities. Recently a certain number of them have published some very remarkable studies on the priesthood in journals initiated for this purpose, and in books reflecting study, experience, zeal, and spirituality.*[14]

This part, treating the formation of the priest as another Christ-Priest by Mary, will not repeat what others have already stated with exceptional competence. It merely seeks to point out the powerful help close association with Mary, as Mother and Associate of the Christ-Priest, brings to the understanding and practice of priestly obligations, and the holiness expected of priests.

---

14 Cf. the publications of M. l'abbe H. Courtois.

CHAPTER SEVEN

Entrusting Sacerdotal Education to Mary

The role of a mother is not only to give life to a human being but also to nurture it. Every complete mother is an educator. Mary carried all priests in her womb and gave birth to them as she gave birth to the Christ-Priest. She was His educator and should be theirs as well.

Mary prepared Jesus for total sacrifice. She guided the development of His Body which was to be sacrificed on Calvary. She guided the development of His Soul in what pertained to human learning and to the exterior manifestations of religion—formulas and gestures—customary among the faithful Jews of her time.

With regard to His special relation to the Father and His priestly mission, she had nothing to teach Him. The grace of infused knowledge and the beatific vision guided Him with infallible clarity at every step of His way. It was Mary who learned from her Son. However, by her care to dwell lovingly on Jesus' priestly mind-set, she afforded Him the encouragement needed to face a difficult task that comes from a person who understands and is ready to assist.

Priests must learn how to be priests. They are merely surrogates, instruments of the Christ-Priest, but not blind instruments. Christ wishes to use them as ministers who are intelligent, deliberate, free, and responsible—ministers who are resolved to imitate His priestly dispositions as perfectly as possible. It is under the guidance of Mary that they will best learn to reproduce them.

No one knows them better than Mary. She knows them from dwelling on them constantly. She knows them from sharing them with her Son, the Christ-Priest, as they worked together. And she has a special gift for sharing them because God, in willing her to be the Mother of priests, also willed that she be a complete Mother and their educator.

The educator role of an ordinary mother ends when her child becomes an adult. In the case of priests, this role of their heavenly Mother continues until they die because they are always children in the supernatural order. As St. Paul said, and she can say it more truthfully than St. Paul: *My little children, with whom I am again in travail until Christ*—the Christ-Priest—*be formed in you* (Gal 4:19).

Before making a one-by-one study of the priestly dispositions of Jesus *under the guidance of Mary*, we must explain the two conditions which are indispensable if this study is to achieve complete success. They are: a) total consecration to Mary, and b) reflection on the Christ-Priest under the tutelage of Mary.

CHAPTER EIGHT

Total Consecration to Mary

In order to become a priest, the Son of God placed everything in the hands of Mary. He decided to belong to her in the same way every child belongs to its mother—even more so, because He was an only child. He obeyed her. He remained with her until He was thirty years old. He wanted her with Him as He lived out His mysteries. And throughout all eternity, He will be a Son deferring to the wishes of His Mother.

As a special child of Mary, the priest should also place everything in her hands, preferably by an act of total consecration. This is the easiest way and the most perfect way for him to become another Christ-Priest. Such a consecration will assure docility towards his heavenly Educator. This is virtually indispensable because learning to be another Christ-Priest means learning how to cease preoccupation with self, how to refrain from continually seeking one's own interests, how to live only for the Father and for souls, how to surrender oneself as Christ did. To accomplish all this, total consecration to Mary is the surest and most perfect way of doing so.

It goes without saying that Mary is not the ultimate goal of consecration to her. God alone is our final goal. But actual practice demonstrates, and traditional teaching indicates that total consecration to Mary is the best way to attain our purpose in life.

We are speaking here of a *true* consecration. There are pious practices called "consecrations to Mary" which are more a self-seeking than a self-giving. One consecrates a child to Mary or one consecrates oneself to Mary at the time of First Communion or at the end of a parish mission, but it is for the purpose of getting her special protection. Father Zucchi's well-known act of consecration to Mary is an example. After devoutly stating to the Blessed Virgin: "I consecrate to you my eyes, my ears, my mouth, my entire person," the prayer concludes, "Because I belong to you, O my good Mother, guard me and defend me as your possession and your property." It is a most legitimate request, one that pleases the Blessed Virgin and Our Lord, but it is not a donation properly speaking. It is more like a contract—*Do ut des* (I give so that you may give in return)—than a gratuitous gift. Properly speaking, consecration means giving oneself to Mary without any expectation of a return. It is made to please her and to further her interests above all.

There are two leading forms of true total consecration to Mary. The best known is that of "holy slavery in regard to Mary" or "holy slavery in regard to Jesus through Mary" taught by the great servant of Mary, St. Louis Marie de Montfort. It is possible that, after the Bible and the *Imitation of Christ,* no book has had as many copies printed as did *True Devotion to the Blessed Virgin*, which explains his teaching.

There is another form of true, total consecration to Mary, which is rapidly becoming better known. It is that taught by Blessed William Joseph Chaminade, founder of several Marian organizations and two religious congregations: the Institute of the Daughters of Mary and the Society of Mary (Marianists). Blessed Chaminade was unaware of the treatise on holy slavery but he likewise taught a total consecration of self to Mary, affirmed by a special vow in both his religious congregations. The form he promoted emphasized two principal features: the imitation of Jesus' filial piety towards His Mother and an apostolic character, a total giving of self to her in her mission of overcoming Satan especially in these modern times.[15]

Whatever form of total consecration one chooses, it is important that it be *lived*. This means that one no longer conducts oneself as proprietor and master of self, of what one has and of what one does, but as someone who belongs completely and irrevocably to Mary. As a consequence, one administers one's wealth in accord with the known or surmised intentions of Mary and uses one's body in accord with her wishes. It means that one does not voluntarily occupy oneself with any thoughts, aspirations, inclinations or decisions other than

---

15 Cf. la Doctrine Mariale de M. Chaminade, Editions du Cerf by E. Neubert. Cf. also Neubert's Mon Ideal, Jesus, Fils de Marie, Editions Mappus, Le Puy. An edition in English of this book under the title: My Ideal—Jesus, Son of Mary is available from TAN Books and Publishers, Inc., P.O. Box 424, Rockford IL 61105. This book explains total consecration in a form adapted to the general faithful.

those of which Mary approves. It means that one does what Mary wants one to do.

To live a complete belonging to Mary faithfully, it is necessary to renew one's consecration to her very often, especially in circumstances that require a particularly difficult sacrifice. Practical suggestions for living out and renewing total consecration to Mary can be found in two books: *True Devotion to the Blessed Virgin* and *My Ideal, Jesus, Son of Mary*. Also helpful are prayers to Our Lord for the grace of imitating his filial piety towards His Mother.[16]

CHAPTER NINE

Daily Reflection with Mary on the Christ-Priest

It is the function of Mary, Mother and Educator, to help priests understand the Christ-Priest. To do this properly, she needs to give them lessons

---

[16] Cf. the prayer of St. Ambrose in the appendix of *My Ideal—Jesus, Son of Mary*. Also note the suggestion of St. John Eudes: "Ask Jesus to love Mary with his heart and ask Mary to love Jesus with her heart."

regularly; she gives these lessons during their daily mental prayer. It is only then, during immediate, personal, and loving contemplation of the Christ-Priest, that they will learn to *sentire in nobis quod et in Christo Jesu sacerdote* (experience within themselves what Jesus Christ, the Priest, experiences).

The recitation of the Divine Office from the breviary and the celebration of the Sacrifice of the Mass are, in themselves, more sacred than mental prayer. But without mental prayer, the Divine Office quickly becomes a tiresome duty, performed hastily and mechanically. Without it, the celebration of the Mass becomes a mere ceremony, more important than other ones perhaps, but carried out coldly and inattentively, disquieting the faithful.

Contrariwise, mental prayer helps a priest—praying the psalms in imitation of Jesus, Mary and Joseph, who prayed them regularly—to find therein a rich source of understanding and inspiration. Doing so, he learns how to bring to God his problems, his fears, his failings as well as his love, his commitment, and his desire to know and carry out God's will.

Thanks to mental prayer, the celebration of Holy Mass increasingly becomes a way in which the priest transforms himself into Jesus, Priest and Victim. He is enabled to set aside pettiness and personal worries, and offer with Christ the Sacrifice of Calvary for the salvation of the world; to immolate himself with Christ for souls, and to feel within himself a new strength and a new courage for facing the tasks and difficulties of each day.

There are priests who claim that the preparation of homilies and other instructions as well as the various functions of their ministry, provide for them the equivalent of mental prayer. But as St. Pius X remarked in his *Letter to Catholic Priests*: "When priests, who do not regularly commune with God, speak to others about Him or give instructions in the Catholic Faith, the Holy Spirit does not breathe for them and, in their hands, the Gospel becomes lifeless. Their voices, however powerful, knowledgeable or eloquent they may be, are not the voice of the Good Shepherd whose sheep listen and follow. They are merely empty noises and passing fads... It is the same all their lives. They do not produce good fruit, at least not lasting fruit."

A priest who does not practice mental prayer becomes a robot performing a number of sacred actions or a recorder repeating ritual words. He gives no spiritual help to the faithful or to himself. He gives the impression that he is a mere functionary and sometimes makes people wonder whether he really believes what he says.

The Church is aware of the great importance of mental prayer for a priest. Canon Law formally recommends this for all of them. "Let the Bishops take great care that all their clergy…devote a certain period of time to mental prayer each day."[17] In *Menti nostrae*, his exhortation to all the clergy, Pope Pius XII unequivocally stresses its value. He writes:

> Above all else, the Church exhorts us to the practice of meditation, which raises the mind to the contemplation of heavenly things, which infuses the heart with love of God and guides it on the straight path to Him. The meditation on sacred things offers the best means of preparation before, and thanksgiving after, the celebration of the Eucharistic Sacrifice. Meditation also disposes the soul to savor and to comprehend the beauties of the Liturgy and leads us to the

---

17 Father Neubert is quoting canon 125 of the 1917 Code of Canon Law. This Code was in force until November 27, 1983 when it was replaced by a new Code. Canon 276 of the new Code says: "They (the priests) are exhorted to engage regularly in mental prayer, to approach the sacrament of penance frequently, to honor the Virgin Mother of God with particular veneration, and to use other general and special means to holiness."

contemplation of the eternal verities, and of the marvelous examples and teachings of the Gospels.

It behooves the sacred ministers, therefore, to strive to reproduce in themselves the examples of the Gospels and the virtues of the divine Redeemer… The priest cannot acquire dominion over himself and his senses, cannot purify his spirit, and cannot strive for virtue as he should. In brief, he cannot faithfully, generously, or fruitfully fulfill the duties of his sacred ministry, unless his life becomes one with the life of the Lord through assiduous and unceasing meditation on the mysteries of the divine Redeemer, the supreme model of perfection and the inexhaustible source of sanctity.

We, therefore, consider it our grave duty to exhort you in a special manner to the practice of daily meditation…for just as the desire for priestly perfection is nourished and strengthened by daily meditation, so its neglect is the source of distaste for spiritual things, through which piety is lessened and grows languid, and the impulse towards personal sanctification is not only weakened or ceases altogether, but the entire priestly ministry suffers great harm. It must, therefore, be stated without reservation that no other means has the unique efficacy of meditation, and that as a consequence, its daily practice can in nowise be substituted for.[18]

Some priests might object that they have so many things to do they have no time for meditation. One always finds the time to do what one considers most important. Neglecting meditation means one considers it less important than other things. No matter how pressing and how numerous one's obligations, there always seems to be a moment or two or three to sit down to eat. The soul needs nourishment as well as the body.

Priests should imitate the apostles. To find time for prayer and for preaching, they delegated administrative tasks to assistants. ...*Pick out... men...whom we may appoint to this duty...we will devote ourselves to prayer and to the ministry of the word* (Acts 6:3–4). Let priests involve the laity according to their abilities. In doing so, they will involve them more significantly in the life of the Christian community. As for those matters they cannot delegate, they should give priority to their

---

18 Menti nostrae, nn. 46–48.

meditation and do the best they can with the time remaining.

Experience will teach priests, as it has so many others, that when they begin their day with this intimate dialogue with Jesus, they will carry out their required responsibilities more quickly and with greater success. This is because they will avoid the loss of time brought on by anxiety or lack of focus. God will be acting in them. No one did a better job of finding time to initiate and sustain religious foundations, to convert hosts of sinners, to lead to perfection large groups of dedicated souls than Dominic, Francis, Ignatius of Loyola, Teresa of Avila and so many others who dedicated several hours each day to meditation.

Mary was a contemplative soul. She wants priests to imitate her. It is only in this way that she can help them to take on the spirit of the Christ-Priest. Total consecration to her, even that sealed by a vow, will not suffice.

Priests, then, should include at least a half hour of morning meditation in their daily schedules and, if possible, another half hour in the evening. For them to reject this necessary practice is tantamount to a refusal to become an authentic priest of Christ. It is the acceptance of a calculated risk of perhaps abandoning a great number of souls they might have won for Jesus, had they heeded the urging of the Holy Father and adopted the indispensable practice of mental prayer.

CHAPTER TEN

Meditating on the Christ-Priest with Mary

The goal of a priest's meditation is to learn how to think, feel, decide, act, and suffer as Christ did. Not the Christ who is a model of perfection for a person in religious life, but the Christ-Priest who is the Mediator between God and His creatures. It is this difference that makes his meditation priestly.

The way to achieve this identification is a trusting and loving union with Jesus in Mary's presence, with her help. This union with Christ has an astonishing power to sanctify and transform for natural and supernatural reasons.

First of all, for natural reasons: To successfully model oneself on another it is necessary to study this other person as closely and as often as possible.

Best results come when the model is a living person. Contact with an individual possessing a strong and engaging personality effects an irresistible influence on those who love, admire, and stay in close contact with him. His ways of thinking, feeling, and deciding are transmitted to them. There is a sort of spiritual transfusion of the dispositions of his soul into theirs.

No individual ever possessed a personality as powerful and as engaging as that of Jesus. No individual was ever loved and admired as much as He was. In His presence, no one could escape His influence. Crowds followed Him everywhere, even into the desert, oblivious of their hunger (cf. Mk 6:31–44; 8:1–10). Even His enemies admitted: *No man ever spoke like this man* (Jn 7:46).

Secondly, for supernatural reasons: The humanity of Christ functioned *ex opere operato*, as it were, like a sacrament. On one occasion, when a sick woman touched the fringe of His garment and was cured, He asked, *Who was it that touched me?... I perceive that power has gone forth from me* (Lk 8:45–46). Saint Luke, who related this incident, had previously pointed out concerning the many sick people who came to Jesus, *...power came forth from him and healed them all* (Lk 6:19). It is always the same. Power emanates from Him, healing and sanctifying all who approach Him with faith and love.

Experience has shown that a mere half hour of intimate union with Jesus brings about greater progress in humility, patience, etc., than ten hours of intellectual reflection on these virtues. It goes without saying that the more trusting and loving this union is, the more smoothly this transfusion of virtues flows from the soul of Christ into the soul of a disciple.

Numerous explanations and experiences have shown the importance of entering into this union with Jesus in the company of Mary. These will be specified further on. For the moment, it suffices to quote the categorical statement of St. Pius X in his encyclical, *Ad diem illum*: "Since it has pleased eternal Providence to give us the God-Man through the Blessed Virgin and since she, having been made fruitful by the Holy Spirit, formed him in her womb, what is more natural for us than to receive Christ from the hands of Mary?... No one in the world knows Jesus better than she does; no one is a better tutor or a better guide for making Jesus known. Consequently, no one is her equal in promoting union with Jesus." Thus it is easy to understand that if we go to Jesus with Mary and feel her close to us as we converse with Him, our union with Him will be more trusting, more loving, more intimate and, as a result, more efficacious.

A heart-to-heart encounter with Jesus is more easily accomplished before the Blessed Sacrament. There, one is in the presence of the same Christ, Son of God and Son of Mary, who attracted crowds of followers; who taught, healed, pardoned, captivated, renewed, and finally gave His life for all men and women. When possible, it is preferable to make one's meditation in a church or chapel, but if this is not convenient, then in that secret chapel found in each of us. Recall the advice Our Lord gave to St. Catherine of Siena when her mother forbade her to visit the church. He told her to build a chapel in her heart where she would always find Him. A habit of meeting with Jesus in this personal sanctuary promotes a spirit of prayer and greater union with Him.

Generally, and especially in the beginning, a priest should strive to acquire a particular virtue of the Christ-Priest, one that he lacks most of all or one that circumstances indicate he should acquire. He might recall a passage of the Gospel, or some word or action of Jesus that manifests this virtue. But this word or action should not be a pretext for searching in one's mind or in some book for indications of this virtue's importance, nature, or practice. There is no point in searching for Jesus in lukewarm or muddy waters. He himself is the gushing fountainhead of living water. He is the book that will teach the priest everything. Stay close to Him.

When I am in His gentle presence, I realize that this word or action of Christ is meant for me. Or, to put it more aptly, during meditation one does not speak *about* Jesus; one speaks *to* Jesus:

> Jesus, there in the tabernacle, or here in my heart, which I am offering or will soon offer to your Father, it is for me that you have spoken this word or performed this action. What exactly do you wish me to learn? In what way do you understand this virtue you are asking me to take on? In what way is it important as you see it? In what way is it important for me?

> You care for this virtue. Why?... Because it gives glory to your Father? Because it serves the salvation of men and women?... Because it helps me follow in your footsteps? You have practiced this virtue at all times, often paying a high price for doing so. You wish me to do the same. I will try to do so. I am afraid. But you wish it. I want to love you, to love your Father, to save the souls you bring to

me. I must think, and love, and live as you did so that you can continue your priesthood through me.

I listen to Him, I revere Him, I love Him, I submit to His request. I make acts of faith in what He has told me—slowly and deliberately—so that His thought, His love, His desire can penetrate to the very core of my soul. I ask Him for the grace to believe more firmly and more realistically. I ask for the grace to express my appreciation, my gratitude, and my desire to make His dispositions my own. I also ask for the grace to acknowledge my weakness, my insufficiency, my fears, and my confidence that He will make me strong with His strength, make me humble with His humility, make me patient with His patience.

Meditation is not a torrent of chatter. Sentences are rare; only a few seemingly unconnected words: "Jesus, I believe! Jesus, mercy! Jesus, thank You! Have pity! Help me!" Often it is only His name. Thoughts are not expressed. He understands. Sometimes there is only a silence of admiration and love. A silence to listen and to hear what He might have to say.

Thus, in an exchange of thoughts and feelings with Jesus, one begins to somewhat understand the priestly soul of Jesus, to embrace the humility, the patience, the forgetfulness of self so contrary to one's natural tendencies. A bit of Jesus' soul enters one's own soul and this is sufficient for becoming a changed person.

And where is Mary all this time? The requirements for clarity of explanation necessitate separating things which are commingled in reality.

Mary is always present. She is there, not in full view, but as a nearby *felt* presence.

What she learned from observing and listening to Jesus at Nazareth, what she discovered from His followers, and especially what she came to know from the beloved disciple after the death of Jesus, she continually pondered in her heart. And these reflections had a sacerdotal character because she knew she was to be associated with her Son in His Sacrifice. She understood Jesus better than anyone ever did. She identified with His thoughts and feelings, penetrating to the very core of His soul.

If I decide to meditate on some priestly virtue of Christ or on some particular passage of the Gospel, I can be sure Mary did it before I ever did, and immeasurably better than I ever could. She can help me understand a little of what she understood, request what she requested, emulate what she emulated. Without her help, I will remain on the surface of Jesus; with it, I will penetrate His heart. I will understand Him better, love Him better, and have a greater desire to imitate Him because Mary is with me. She will enable me to see Jesus with her eyes, understand Jesus with her mind, and love Him with her heart. By means of her Immaculate Heart, I will absorb from the Sacred Heart of Jesus, His priestly qualities.

Jesus is both God and man. I am but a mere human creature. But Mary, who is also a mere human creature, will show me by her example how to imitate the priestly qualities of Jesus. She who is "pure capacity for Jesus" will show me how to draw from Him as much as I can.

That is why, after having reflected on Jesus, I can turn my attention to her without leaving His presence to see how she imitated Him. This glance does more than give me a better understanding of Jesus. The captivating charm of my Mother, my love for her, my desire to please her by emulating her, drives me to take on, as she did, the qualities of Jesus.

From time to time, I will speak to her as I did to Jesus with simple words or voicing her name: Mary! Or: Mother! She, too, understands what I wish to say. With her, I speak to Jesus. With her,

I speak to the Father, asking him to show me his Son, who is Son of Both. With her, I speak to the Holy Spirit, whose Spouse she is, asking him to help me fully understand and love what Jesus teaches me. Sometimes St. Joseph is also present. He is always at home with Jesus and Mary.

With Mary, it is possible to dwell for hours on Jesus as Priest. One does not intellectualize; one scarcely speaks. One ponders, admires, loves, and changes.

Some distractions come to disturb the conversation. Instead of fighting them, one goes to Mary and, with her, to Jesus. As a result, one continues to pay attention to Him and to love Him. Sometimes they are prolonged, even voluntary. Sometimes one feels too unworthy to converse so familiarly with Jesus because of laziness, or because of a refusal to make a sacrifice or an effort He requested, or because of an offense or a fault. Even so, go to Him, confess the rudeness or the fault and, in spite of it, tell Him of unwavering trust, for if our affliction is great, His mercy is even greater. Remember the confidence of the publican, the prodigal son, the sinful woman, the good thief. Remember the joy He receives from a humble confession.

We will give Him even greater joy if we add to these sentiments of humility and confidence, union with Mary. If, after having committed some fault, we come to Jesus with our Mother, our sorrow and our confidence will always give Him great pleasure, even greater than if we come as a result of a great act of mortification or having recited long supplementary prayers. In this way, we restore intimate, trusting, and loving contact with Him and her.

Sometimes, without any apparent reason, one enters a state of dryness or depression. The thought of Jesus, even in the company of His Mother, leaves one's heart completely indifferent. *Blessed are those who believe without having seen* (Jn 20:29) or sensed. In spite of the emptiness, declare faith in His love and in all that His Mother says of His mercy and goodness. Remain at prayer because that pleases Him even though you are bored. Abiding this way in the presence of Jesus and Mary gives one no consolation, but it gives Jesus great contentment. And knowing Jesus is content brings about great peace in the depths of one's soul.

No matter how productive one's person-to-person conversation with Jesus and Mary may be, it is but a single meditation on the virtue one seeks to acquire from Him. To acquire it as a habitual practice, it is necessary to contemplate the Master over and over. One can always find words and actions of Jesus relating to this virtue. Jesus always spoke and acted as a *priest* and so, in nearly every portion of the Gospel, He is found giving lessons in humility, in forgetfulness of self, in charity, etc. As is the case with mankind's masterpieces, and even more so in the case of Christ, one can scrutinize them over and over again and always discover something new to admire, to love, and to imitate. Mary can never exhaust defining her Son or conclude revealing how to imitate Him.

At times, instead of taking the Gospel as the subject of meditation, one may prefer to dwell on an experience or on an article of faith. But this should always be as Jesus sees it or reflects upon it. In this way it is always Jesus, united with His Mother that one is contemplating.

Once in a while, one may choose to make the Blessed Virgin the subject of a meditation. Everything about Mary relates to Jesus. Her virtues are reproductions of His virtues. Her privileges are participations in His privileges. Her interests are His interests. Everything about her is explained by Jesus' love for her and her love for Jesus. It is always necessary to see her in the light of Jesus. Nothing gives her greater pleasure than making her feastdays occasions for a better understanding of and a greater love for Jesus.

Meditation should infuse a priest's entire day. This hour or half hour of close contact with the Christ-Priest should teach a priest how to act as a priest in everything he does.

Before ending a meditation, try to determine with Mary, in what way and at what particular moments one will try to reproduce the virtue observed in Her Son. Entreat her, submit to her some resolution to be taken, request her help in bringing about its actualization.

During the day, at preset times or at random moments and always in the loving presence of Jesus and Mary, determine as closely as possible how well one tried to imitate the humble Jesus or the patient Jesus. Seek to know why one's efforts fell short or why they were completely lacking. In the evening, try with Mary to foresee at a given moment or in a particular circumstance, how to do better. Again, as in the morning meditation, ask her help, defer to her and entrust your resolve to her. Before retiring for the night a similar review with her is advisable.

This is the way Mary educates a priest. She carries him in her womb until he becomes another Christ-Priest. Happy the priest who is her docile student and happy those souls that he, in turn, helps to imitate Jesus and Mary.[19]

CHAPTER ELEVEN

Acquiring Spiritual Composure with Mary

Meditation should continue beyond the times set for this exercise and infuse daily activities with a spirit of prayer or spiritual composure. Otherwise, its effect is greatly compromised. Adversely, the lack of habitual spiritual composure makes meditation difficult. Even worse, the lack of spiritual composure often makes it difficult to find time for meditation.

---

[19] The ordinary goal of meditation is not to discover new truths, but to help us live truths already known in a new way and in the manner of Christ. However, it is important to plumb the wells of spiritual truth constantly. This is important for a priest, partly to give him new insights as he contemplates the dispositions of Christ and partly to enrich his priestly activities. Constant renewal is needed to maintain unflagging zeal for doing good. Hence, the necessity for fifteen or thirty minutes of daily spiritual reading. We find the time to read the daily news to learn about transient matters. Should we not also find the time to read about eternal ones?

It results in abandoning the practice altogether after a few attempts and in dubbing it a waste of time.

Spiritual composure is necessary from an apostolic point of view as well. *Abide in me, and I in you,* Jesus said to His apostles at the Last Supper. *As the branch cannot bear fruit by itself, unless it abides in the vine…He who abides in me, and I in him, he it is that bears much fruit, for apart from me you can do nothing* (Jn 15:4–5).

To abide in Christ means, first of all, to be in the state of grace. But for us *to bear much fruit,* it is not sufficient for Christ to abide in us as a prisoner in a cell as it were. We must allow Him to act freely in us, to take possession of us, to have us live out His thoughts, feelings, and desires. Because all our capability in the supernatural order comes from Him, we must be firmly united to this source to function there. If we are not connected to the dynamo, we are bulbs that do not give light, motors that do not run. It is in spiritual composure that we have this connection.

The soul of a priest who lacks spiritual composure is a marketplace absorbed in displays and mongering. Such a priest lives according to sensory impressions and rationalization. He does not live by faith. It is not the spirit of Jesus but his own thinking that drives him. His mood varies according to his stamina or the things he finds agreeable or unpleasant. He commits a clutter of faults of which he is scarcely aware, faults he never corrects. He celebrates his Mass and carries out various sacred activities without putting his heart into them, often exhibiting a shocking indifference. He cannot find the time for meditation, particular examen, spiritual reading, the Rosary, or for carrying out the obligations of his ministry as he should. He preaches properly, even brilliantly, but what one hears is a man more or less gifted in turning a phrase—not the voice of God! His ministry is marked by many popular activities but it is all noise and glamour, producing no supernatural results. He does not succeed in putting souls in contact with Christ.

The priest who is spiritually composed lives, as much as possible, in the sanctuary of his soul with Our Lord and the Holy Trinity. He thinks and acts in faith. The Holy Spirit directs him and regularly helps him understand what he must do and what he must avoid. He is self-possessed and understands himself. He is aware of temptations stemming from sinful nature, even the most subtle ones, and he resists them. He is aware of his dangerous tendencies and controls them. When he is thwarted or treated unjustly, he remains in a God-given peace. People unacquainted with him recognize him as a man of God when they observe him celebrating Mass or performing some priestly ministry. Even those who meet him on the street are struck by the simple dignity of his manner. He is unflustered by a heavy workload because he avoids useless diversions and because two are undertaking it—God and himself. He may not be gifted with great eloquence but his words are effective. A simple statement or a bit of homely advice from him is more persuasive than another's brilliant discourse. It is Christ speaking through him.

It is clear that spiritual composure must be learned at the school of Jesus and Mary. From the first moment of His conception, Christ in His humanity, was aware of His union with the Eternal Word and, from then on, beheld God uninterruptedly. While Jesus worked with His father at Nazareth, while He preached to the crowds and debated with the scribes and Pharisees, even while He slept, His soul contemplated the Father and conversed with Him. From time to time, He set aside all other matters and gave complete attention to the Father. This occurred often during the thirty years of His hidden life, during the forty days He fasted in the desert, and even during the period of His ministry when

He retired to a mountain solitude to spend a night in prayer.

To the extent that the life of a mere human being can resemble that of a humanity hypostatically united to the Divinity, the interior life of Mary surely resembled that of her Son. She did not enjoy the beatific vision,[20] but hers was a vision of God more perfect than that of the greatest mystics. She was able to know God from the moment of her conception thanks to infused knowledge and, thereby, to respond to the infinite love of the Father with an ineffably tender and ardent filial love. Before coming to know the world-at-large, she communicated with the supernatural world in a most wholesome and abiding interchange. At an early age, she devoted herself to the exclusive service of God by a vow of virginity. While it is improbable that she spent some years in the Temple at Jerusalem,[21] her own soul was the Holy of Holies in which she communed with God night and day. In the antiphon for the *Magnificat* on the feast of the Presentation of Mary in the Temple, the Liturgy states: "Holy Mother of God, Mary ever-Virgin,

---

[20] This is not the place to discuss the question as to whether or not she was ever favored with this vision.

[21] Cf. Vie de Marie by E. Neubert, Editions Salvator, second edition, pp. 9–14.

you are the temple of the Lord and the dwelling place of the Holy Spirit. Beyond all others you were pleasing to our Lord Jesus Christ." Certain mystics (St. Teresa of Avila, for example) were conscious of God even during their sleep. *A fortiori* we can affirm the same of Mary.

On two occasions, Saint Luke describes Mary as pondering in her heart all that she heard about her Son. The same writer tells us of the presence of the Mother of God in the Upper Room during the ten days of prayer that preceded the coming of the Holy Spirit (cf. Acts 1:14). Can Mary be understood other than as one in constant communion with the Divinity? In the former breviary prayers for the feast of the Assumption, the Church attributed to Mary the words of Christ concerning another Mary, the one who sat at the Lord's feet and listened to His teaching: *[She] has chosen the good portion, which shall not be taken away from her* (Lk 10:42).

Do not, however, picture Mary in a constant state of ecstasy and out of touch with the material world. Mary was never in ecstasy. Ecstasy indicates a mystical union still imperfect. She devoted herself completely to the duties of a young girl and then to those of a mother, wife and housekeeper. The Gospels indicate that these left her little time for rest. In carrying out even the most mundane of these demanding duties, she remained in deep contemplation of the Divinity. Souls who have reached the highest state of mystical life do the same. Whether she was working, praying, listening, speaking, presenting herself in the Temple, or fleeing to Egypt, she was absorbed in Jesus. Thus every occupation, even those most disconcerting, led her to Him.

If we place ourselves under the guidance of Mary, she will teach us how to live an interior life like her own. To do this, we must agree to remove all the obstacles that impede us from entering the sanctuary in our souls where God abides. These are all the images and thoughts that flood our minds when we allow our senses to hear, to see, and to read everything that can satisfy an idle curiosity. Excessive chit-chat with others can also be an obstacle. What would the Blessed Virgin do in our place? Imitate her!

No matter how captivating they may be, we must banish from our minds all the memories, thoughts, images, and dreams that have nothing to do with the work at hand. Mary was always concerned for God's will in regard to the present moment. She left the past in God's hands and trusted in Him for the future.

Whenever we are dominated by some emotion—joy, sadness, fear, anger, rebellion, or rancor—we must restore peace of mind as quickly as possible. Simply bring the emotion to the Blessed Virgin's attention and, with her, search for its cause. Ordinarily, it is some form of self-seeking. Reaffirm total consecration to her telling her: "Mother, I am all yours. I want to do and to undergo all that you wish me to. Give me the strength I need." If we are sincere, that will restore our peace of mind.

To put it in a nutshell, interior silence must be developed most of all. Anyone who fails to be composed will never hear God speaking deeply within to enlighten him, to animate him, to reform him, and through Him, to reform many others.

All of this is more or less negative work. There must also be positive union with God. As did Jesus and Mary, we must retire for reflection into that secluded place in our souls where the Holy Trinity dwells. We cannot see God directly as Our Lord did in His humanity. We cannot be uninterruptedly conscious of God as the Blessed Virgin was. But we know from our Faith that God dwells in our souls, that it is no longer we who live, that it is Christ who lives in us. We must make multiple acts of faith in this special presence of God. Loving acts of faith in the belief that a loving God is constantly within us to heap his gifts upon us, cannot fail to invigorate and gladden us.

It is appropriate to meditate frequently on this mysterious presence of God in our souls, repeating this practice throughout each day. Eventually, it will become automatic. If it is with Mary that we adore God within us, and if it is with her that we express our love and our needs, the thought of this presence of God will become more and more encouraging and engaging, more and more personal and familiar, and consequently more and more natural and rewarding. By recalling this presence with Mary each time we pray, our prayers will be less of a mechanical recitation of formulas and more and more a lively conversation with the Father, or the Son, or the Holy Spirit, or all three together.

For a Marian devotee, there is also a living in the presence of Mary. She is not within us as God is, but she sees us, hears us, and assists us more perfectly than anyone on earth. She is that close to us. A blind and deaf child does not perceive its mother directly, but is aware of her presence by the soft and loving hand that fondles him, comforts him, feeds him, and tends to his every need. In our relation to Mary we are like that blind and deaf child, but we are aware of her presence in a different way. Some mystics are habitually conscious of Mary's influence in their lives. It is easy to imagine what mastery the awareness of Mary's presence can bring to a life of spiritual composure.

In a very active life like that of a priest, it is generally impossible to devote long periods of time to quiet communion with Our Lord and His Mother. Torn in all directions by his multiple duties, how can he maintain a life of spiritual composure? If it is a question of *his* duties, that is, of functions he performs *in his own name*, such a life is impossible. But if it is a question of functions carried out for Jesus and Mary, there is little difficulty entailed. We have seen that the duties of Mary did not distract her from the thought of Jesus because it was for Him that she did everything. Everything a priest does should be done to promote the interests of Jesus. Before undertaking any activity, the priest who imitates his Mother will decide with her how to please Jesus in carrying it out. By striving to remain united to Him as he works, the priest will find that the work keeps Jesus on his mind. An easy way to maintain the loving thought of Jesus and Mary during any activity is to invoke their names from time to time. Saying, "Jesus" unites us with Mary and saying "Mary" or "Mother" unites us with Jesus if we speak these names with the love Jesus had for His Mother and the love Mary had for her Son.

It happens all too frequently that distractions, more or less voluntary (a bit of self-seeking or an outright misdeed), will lead us away from Jesus and Mary. Without giving way to discouragement and without making efforts to chase away these distractions and moments of self-concern, go directly to Jesus with Mary, our help and our security, and you will be quickly restored to their loving presence.

Fidelity to these practices will unite the priest more and more to the Christ-Priest and to His Mother and Associate. It will no longer be the priest who ministers to souls; it will be Him and her. And if he gives them free reign to act through him, what marvels will take place!

CHAPTER TWELVE

Mary Teaches the Priest How to Live by Faith

In His final appearance to His apostles Jesus told them, *Go into all the world and preach the*

Gospel to the whole creation. He who believes and is baptized will be saved; but he who does not believe will be condemned (Mk 16:15–16). The mission of the priest is to spread the Faith and, thereby, save the world.

This ever-important mission is particularly so at the present time. There are still thousands of pagans in the world. And the great scandal of the Church today is that a multitude of individuals whose ancestors were fervent Christians have lost their faith. Even among those calling themselves believers, there are a great number who think and feel, judge and act, like the unbelievers around them. Is there any difference between them other than attending Mass on Sunday and receiving the sacraments at Easter time?

There are even many priests who speak, judge, and act as if they had never read the Gospel. Christ told His priests, *You are the salt of the earth; but if salt has lost its taste, how shall its saltiness be restored?... You are the light of the world,...but if it is...put under a bushel,...* how can it illumine those still living in darkness? The salt which has lost its saltiness...*is no longer good for anything except to be thrown out and trodden underfoot by men* (Mt 5:13–15). The world is becoming more and more corrupt. Isn't this because the salt has lost its taste?

Isn't it true that ordinary faithful Christians are more often guided by faith in their conduct and decisions than are the priests who are responsible for their care? On a number of occasions, Our Lord praised the faith of humble individuals and complained of the incredulity of those in the priestly ranks. Recall the commendation He gave the woman with the flow of blood (cf. Mk 5:34), His tributes to the centurion (cf. Mt 8:10), and the Canaanite woman (cf. Mt 15:28). Then recall the reproaches He addressed to the apostles during the storm on the lake, *Why are you afraid? Have you no faith?* (Mk 4:40). After asking them, *O men of little faith, why do you discuss among yourselves the fact that you have no bread?* Jesus warned them, *Be on your guard against the leaven of the Pharisees* (Mt 16:8, 11). At the time the apostles were unable to remove the evil spirit from the epileptic child *because of* [their] *lack of faith* (Mt 17:19), He exclaimed, *O faithless and perverse generation, how long am I to bear with you?* (Mt 17:17). Recall that when Jesus reached out and caught Peter trying to walk on water He asked, *O man of little faith, why did you doubt?* (Mt 14:31).

It was not that the apostles had no faith at all but, that, called to transmit the Faith, they were expected to have greater faith than others. The same applies to priests. If they are not men of faith, what are they? They are like the hypocrites about whom Jesus declared: *The scribes and Pharisees sit on Moses' seat; so practice and observe whatever they tell you, but not what they do; for they preach, but do not practice* (Mt 23:2–3). There is a saying: "Nothing is so pernicious as good advice followed by a bad example." If a priest does not live according to the Faith he preaches, he risks destroying it in the hearts of his listeners. On the other hand, if he practices all that he preaches, his conduct will strengthen the faith of believers and render unbelievers more pensive than any eloquent sermon could.

Perhaps we believe ourselves men of faith. We do not doubt any declaration of Christ or any article of the Creed. That is speculative faith.

But do we have practical faith? A spirit of faith? Think for a moment. With regard to truths that require no sacrifice (the Real Presence, the Trinity, heaven) there is no difficulty. But what about truths that entail some cost? Do we see God in our superiors or merely a man? Do we see Jesus Christ, who shed His Blood for them, in impious Christians, in unbelievers, in enemies of the Church? When we visit the sick, we see the malady as God's will and remain unperturbed. But when someone's stupidity or malice harms us, do we see it as God's loving will for us, or only as someone's idiocy or perverseness?

When we do not know where to find the resources needed for the future, do we lose our peace of mind or do we tell ourselves that our heavenly Father knows our plight and will come to our aid when needed?

Read the eight Beatitudes again, not to see how they pertain to others but to see how they apply to you. If you are poor, hungry, or persecuted, or if you are hated, insulted or scorned, do you ever think about praying a *Magnificat* to thank God for including you in the Beatitudes? Read the Gospels slowly, from beginning to end. Each time you hear Christ counseling something, ask yourself if you think or act as He advised. Perhaps you will say that these counsels must be interpreted in an accommodated sense. Did the saints do that? Were not the great apostles who changed the world those who followed the injunctions of the Gospel literally? Christians are losing their faith because their priests lack it. It is by the power of faith that the masses will be converted, that obstacles will be overcome, and its enemies defeated. It is all important that one's faith be lived and constantly grow.

Who will be the model for this life of faith? Not Christ; He did not have faith—he saw! It is Mary, proclaimed blessed by the Holy Spirit because she believed (cf. Lk 1:45). Reflect on her often and with love. What heroic faith she needed to accept and to live out the tutelage of God. The angel told her she was to be the Mother of the Messiah—not the Messiah expected by the Jewish people, a mere man gifted with a special power from heaven— but Mother of the Son of God, Messiah by an unprecedented virgin birth. And this poor young girl of Nazareth scarcely fifteen years old simply believed and spoke her *fiat*.

This Messiah, the Son of God, was born in Bethlehem. She carried Him to His own people, but they did not accept Him. Almost immediately, the King of the Jews forced the Son of God to flee to Egypt in the arms of His mother. It was the will of God. Mary believed and obeyed. For thirty years He lived at her side, learning Joseph's line of work, laboring hard for a meager livelihood. Was this the way to save His people and teach all nations? Mary believed and waited.

Then He sets out to preach and work His miracles. Crowds follow Him with enthusiasm. But soon some Pharisees and priests, people who should be helping Him, turn the people against Him by lies and threats. He, the Son of God, is condemned as a blasphemer and hung from a cross between two thieves. Mary remains at His side. The angel had told her, *God will give him the throne of David, his father* (Lk 1:32). Is this horrible gibbet David's throne? *He will reign over the house of Jacob forever* (Lk 1:33). Will He who is crying out in agony reign forever? The faith of the apostles crumbles; Mary's faith remains steadfast.

At the side of our Mother we will learn to live our Faith. A life lived in union with Mary develops a deep spirit of faith intuitively. Fervent members of the faithful, who call to mind the central mysteries of the Faith as they pray their rosaries, live their faith each day better than priests who cannot find the time to do the same.

These practical measures should be followed regularly:

—Listen carefully to Jesus speaking in the Gospels.

—Frequently ask, especially when facing difficulties, "What would Jesus and Mary think or do?"

—Make frequent acts of faith: "Jesus, I believe; increase my faith."

—Not only confess the Faith; love it! Jesus teaches through love.

—Harmonize conduct with convictions for fear of harmonizing convictions with conduct.

—Before any action, consult with Mary to learn how to please Jesus.

—Be ready to endure with love, the pain that comes when facing demanding truths difficult to believe.

—Maintain a stance of faith staying composed, reserved, and modest with Mary beside you and Jesus within you.

—Develop the humility and trust needed to follow the guidance of the Holy Spirit.

—In the face of every difficulty, have recourse to Jesus and to Mary with an unshakable confidence, and experience the supernatural in the resulting triumphs.

This is the victory that overcomes the world, our faith (1 Jn 5:4).

"Mary, most faithful, pray for your priests."

CHAPTER THIRTEEN

Mary Teaches Priestly Self-Denial

Self-denial is an indispensable condition Christ imposes on anyone who wishes to be His disciple (cf. Mt 16:24). It is required of a priest not only because he should be a model disciple but also because it is mandatory for his basic function. The priest is a mediator. A mediator cannot be self-serving. His job is to unite two parties. If he is concerned only for himself, he ceases to be a mediator.

Pagan priests and Jewish Levites were only part-time priests. They had other demanding occupations such as magistrate, military leader, political ruler, or those more prosaic such as farmer, artisan, etc. This is not the case for an individual sharing the priesthood of Christ.

Christ came among us as a priest. On entering this world, He offered Himself to the Father as a victim (cf. Heb 10:5). He lived as a priest with this offering ever in view. He died as a priest in an act of supreme sacrifice. There was not a moment in His life when He was not thinking, judging, or acting as a priest. His purpose was to serve and not to be served (cf. Mt 20:28).

The Catholic priesthood is the extension of the priesthood of Christ and so, like Christ, its members do not have the right to live for themselves. From the moment of their ordination they exist to serve God and souls, and not to be served. If they become self-serving, they cease to act as priests. It is for this reason that Church leadership requires celibacy and rules out purely civil occupations. If they are teachers or writers, it is as priests and in keeping with their priestly mission that they do this. Even when they eat or sleep, they do it as Christ did, to have the strength to carry out their priestly mission.

In the words of Abbe Chevier, "The priest is a man consumed by his career." Father Shellhorn made a similar observation, "A priest is never unavailable." Pope Pius XII urged, "May you one and all, in humility and sincerity, always be able to attribute to yourselves—with your spiritual charges as witnesses—the words of the Apostle, *I will most gladly spend and be spent for your souls* (2 Cor 12:15). Let it always be clear to everybody that the priest, in all his activities, seeks nothing beyond the good of souls, and looks toward no one but Christ to Whom he consecrates his energies and his whole self."[22]

---

22 Menti nostrae, n. 61.

There is yet another reason that requires total self-sacrifice of the priest. As a priest of Christ, he must be a victim with Christ. To be a victim with Christ, he must not only ignore self-seeking, he must make a total sacrifice of himself. A hard saying! Who can accept it?

There are priests for whom the priesthood is a life of happy tranquility which has been awarded them and in which other individuals exist for their benefit. Happily their number is decreasing. There are others who work diligently but, in doing so, seek to satisfy a need for activity, for control, for approbation, for showing compassion, or as a temporary escape from distasteful duty. There are others who have a truly apostolic outlook and who work very hard in the ministry, but then seek to be lavishly rewarded for the efforts they have made. Finally there are those who work only for the good of souls without seeking any exceptional recompense. Just one such priest accomplishes more than a hundred of those who take the ordinary course of action. Their numbers are increasing however, and if they were in the majority, the world would rapidly be transformed!

How is it possible for a priest to achieve this total self-sacrifice so contrary to human nature? It is by meditating, in union with Mary, on the

Christ-Priest. In this meditation with Mary, he will penetrate to the very heart of Jesus. With her, he will come to know the infinite love Christ has for His Father, whose glory He has come to restore, and for all the men and women He wishes to redeem and lead to the Father as other sons and daughters. He will come to understand why Jesus, Mediator between the Father and these other children, must necessarily sacrifice Himself, and why He lovingly embraces this self-sacrifice made on behalf of His Father and the human race. He will see that Jesus is bent upon it out of love for the Father and for us, and is happy to practice it in every circumstance.

With Mary, he will revere this disposition of Jesus, he will cherish it, and he will ask the Master to embed it in his heart so that he can assist in glorifying the Father and in saving souls, no matter what the cost. With Mary, he will reexamine various incidents in the life of Jesus to note how He always conducted Himself as a priest anxious to glorify the Father and to save souls, willingly sacrificing Himself for him and for them. This is evident in His Hidden Life, from the miracles He performed without ostentation on behalf of the unfortunate; in His preaching whereby He sought conversion, not applause; and in His Passion, more concerned for the fate of the pious women who consoled Him than for the compassion they offered Him. Tormented by the hate of His enemies and the desertion of His followers He, nonetheless, speaks words of assurance and consolation to His persecutors whose pardon He requests, to the good thief, to His Mother, to St. John, and to all of us. He is concerned for the prophesies still to be fulfilled (Ps 31; 68) and for the completion of the mission given Him by the Father. He is unmindful of Himself to the very end. *Christus non sibi placuit.*

He will also reflect on Mary, the perfect copy of Jesus in her total self-oblation. Unlike the other children of Adam who begin in self-obsession, she alone, from the moment of her Immaculate Conception, was oriented toward God. She gave herself completely to the Father who made her his beloved daughter. From the first instant of her life until its very end, she remained turned toward God. She was aware of the great things he had done for her, but this knowledge only served to fix her attention more firmly on him who had pity on his chosen creature.

Gabriel informed her that she was to be the Mother of the Messiah, the High Priest who would reconcile the Creator with his creatures. Like Him, she too would be dedicated all her life to the Father and to his unhappy children. *Ecce ancilla*

Domini; fiat mihi secundum verbum tuum. Behold the handmaid of the Lord; let it be to me according to your word (Lk 1:38). She existed for God, for His Son, and for the redemption of sinners. She was not concerned for herself.

She did not explain her miraculous Maternity, even to St. Joseph. God would take care of that. She said nothing to those around her about the wonderful things she knew about Her Son. She was content to appear as an ordinary housewife. The citizens of Nazareth were scandalized to hear Jesus speaking with such authority in their synagogue. *Isn't he the son of Mary?* (Lk 4:22), they asked indignantly. She did not share in the achievements of Jesus; her role was to pray and suffer for Him. We see her at the foot of the Cross. There, a great offering is asked of her: the sacrifice of Her Son and the acceptance of us as her children in His stead. We see her in the Upper Room after the Ascension, but it is Peter who is in charge. She is content to pray with those present. Then, when her earthly mission is completed, she discretely disappears, only to undertake the vastly greater service of all generations until the end of time.

As with Jesus, enter the soul of Mary to see how lovingly she embraced this self-oblation on behalf of the Father and Jesus and souls, and how much happiness it gave her. See also her great desire to inculcate in us this same disposition. Ask the Blessed Mother how to feel and to want what she felt and wanted, and to do so for the same reasons she had. In this close association with Jesus and Mary we will slowly become aware of a personal transformation that mere reasoning and volition cannot bring about.

Total consecration to Mary sincerely made and honestly lived is a powerful help for achieving priestly self-sacrifice. Living this consecration means making use of one's possessions, one's flesh and bones, one's psychic powers (memory, intellect, imagination and will), and one's activity only according to the intentions of Mary, i.e., no longer for oneself but for God. The thought of her, for love of whom this consecration was made, will help us maintain sincerity, and enable us to uncover quickly and surely any secret self-seeking. At the same time, the power of all the graces obtained for us by our Mediatrix will keep us faithful to our self-oblation with little trouble. In this, as with everything else, "every good thing comes to us with her."

CHAPTER FOURTEEN

Acquiring Priestly Humility with Mary

Jesus, meek and humble of heart, make all hearts, especially the hearts of priests, like Thine.

All virtues should be found in priests to a higher degree than usual. Humility, however, should characterize them. Humility is needed by all Christians. Priests need it for a special, priestly reason. It is the very nature of a priest to be a mediator and every mediator is a servant. Servants are subordinate to their masters and are humbly submissive to them. The priest is a mediator between God and men and hence the servant of both.

As a servant of God, the priest must glorify God. One glorifies God by acknowledging one's insignificance as a creature. This humble stance is required of a priest even if the souls he represents have not offended God, but is even more necessary because the glory of God has been outraged by the countless sins of humankind. All these sins are basically sins of pride, refusals to acknowledge God as Sovereign Master. The more humble the priest, the more he glorifies God. The priest who is proud only gives Him displeasure.

As servant of human beings, the priest is expected to obtain God's graces for them and to help them live a holy life. It is Christ he serves in serving souls and, before Christ, he must be humble no matter how excellent his intellectual or social gifts. He is always a priest and, thereby, always a servant. The priest who sees himself serving Christ in his brothers and sisters will feel honored in giving service to them. He will never treat them in a condescending manner. Is a servant ever condescending towards his master? By his attitude toward them, he will give them a sense of their dignity as human beings and as Christians. He is always gracious even toward those who do not agree with him.

In contrast, the priest who is wrapped up in himself and his special gifts,—the priest who is vain and touchy, and especially the priest who is proud—is a priest people shun. They approach him only when they must and they never feel close to God when they are with him. The history of the Church records great apostolic undertakings ruined by a priest's desire for self-glorification. It documents examples of priests who were intelligent, eloquent, capable, successful in winning over many followers, but who ended up in a deplorable state after having caused the Church immense harm, all because they lacked one virtue, that of humility. Even when there is no visible evidence of it, the priest who lacks humility achieves no real good. As Christ has said, *Without me, you can do nothing* (Jn 15:5).

Suppose that, thanks to great effort and sacrifice, we have succeeded in setting in motion an excellent apostolic enterprise which is then destroyed by the lies and insinuations of some jealous person. We of course become indignant at such devilish behavior. But if, in our ministry, we seek our own glory, then it is we who become the satanic destroyer.

As much as it is necessary for a priest to practice humility, it must be pointed out that it is not easy to do so in a satisfactory manner. The avoidance of failings against purity, justice, or patience comes more quickly than failings against humility. We seek excellence and that is good. But if we seek the glory that it gives as if we were the creators of our own excellence, then it is a disorder; or if the excellence is a fiction, it is hypocrisy. In any case, it is a sin against God because it is an attempt to attribute to oneself what is from Him.

A deranged love of glory caused the fall of the angels from heaven and the sin of our first parents. This tendency easily insinuates itself into every human activity, even the holiest, and hides itself under noble pretexts. A priest is always human, a son of our first parents who sought to be God's equal.

There is something worse. The priesthood provides many helps for the practice of other virtues: a sheltering from many occasions of sin and a number of supports provided by God and superiors. For the practice of humility, however, the priesthood involves special obstacles. Every sort of advantage—wealth, knowledge, power—tends to create a corresponding sort of pride. The priest does not escape this law. Called from the ranks of the faithful, he suddenly assumes an elevated status and can speak as one equal to, or even superior to, individuals in all social classes. He is esteemed by the faithful and respected, at least outwardly, by others. If he encounters people who insult him, their hostility makes him feel like a hero persecuted for Christ.

A priest's general education usually exceeds that of most of the faithful he ministers to and his philosophical and theological studies could possibly give him the idea that he possesses infallible truth. And because theology—and wisdom in the form of *philosophia perennis*—judges everything, some priests come to believe they are experts having the last word in a number of related disciplines: psychology, psychiatry, pedagogy, ethics, sociology, fine arts, methodology, etc. It is a professional deformation found in many priests, not so?

The morning after his ordination, the priest experiences members of the faithful, wealthy and poor, educated and unlettered, his seniors and his juniors, submitting to his judgment matters they hide from others (their most secret actions and thoughts), asking his advice on what they have done or what they should do, and requesting absolution. Outside of the confessional, he is consulted on all sorts of other issues. Even in purely secular matters, he often has a greater influence than lay authorities.

Is there a way to avoid savoring one's advantages and misusing them from time to time? Even in the early Church, St. Peter was obliged to warn the priests of his day *not to dominate over those in your charge, but to be examples to the flock* (1Pet 5:3). The faithful and others, accuse priests of many failings against humility: vanity, irritability, jealousy, ambition, arrogance, and taking umbrage at even those well-founded criticisms made by the laity, confreres, and religious or civil authorities.

How can one acquire this virtue of humility, so necessary, but beset with so many difficulties? In the same way one acquires all the other virtues—

by entering the school of Jesus where Mary is the teacher.

Before studying the humility of Jesus and His Mother in what they said and in what they did, it is necessary, first of all, to take note of their fundamental attitude in regard to this virtue.

St. Paul counseled the Philippians: *Have this mind among yourselves, which is yours in Christ Jesus, who, though he was in the form of God, did not count equality with God a thing to be grasped, but emptied himself, taking the form of a servant, being born in the likeness of men. And being found in human form, he humbled himself and became obedient unto death, even death on a cross* (Phil 2:5–8). Christ voluntarily chose this humiliation. Why? It was to redress the pride of disobedient humans and thereby give glory to His Father. At the same time, His humble obedience brought salvation to humankind. He cherished His humiliation, not for itself, but because of what it meant for His Father and for us. In practicing humility, it is the Father and these souls that one must always have in sight. A priest should love humility with the same love he has for God and his fellowmen. If he cherishes it in this way, it will be embraced with joy and it will enable him to avoid with the greatest care any advancement of self as fatal to the accomplishment of the ultimate purpose of his priesthood.

Mary's paramount orientation toward God was inexhaustible love and boundless thanksgiving for the many graces heaped upon her from the first moment of her existence. It was so very clear to her that everything in her came from Him and that, of herself, she was nothing, that the thought of any self-satisfaction seemed completely absurd. Whatever great things the Almighty bestowed on her, she would always be the quiet handmaid of the Lord.

When the Son of God became incarnate in her, she added Christ's paramount orientation to her own. As the Associate of the Christ-Priest, she took on His dispositions toward the Father and toward humankind; her humility became priestly. She embraced this humility with great love as she meditated on the opprobrium of her Son. It made her most happy to be able to give Him the joy of seeing her unite her own humiliations to His and to glorify God with Him, and work for the salvation of souls. No individual ever found as much self-satisfaction in pride as Jesus and Mary found in humiliation.

In studying the humiliations of Jesus and Mary recorded in the Gospels, you must bear in mind their profound motivation regarding humility— their need for it, and their joy when forgotten, misunderstood and abused—before you can imitate them.

There is much in the Scriptures that give us some indication of Jesus and Mary's humility. First of all, during the hidden life: There, the focus is on Mary serving everyone who visits her. She is so simple, so forgetful of herself, so ready to put people at ease. It is as though she was unaware of her dignity. Then, during the public life: Christ preaches and heals, always at everyone's disposal, even those who indiscreetly impede Him from taking a bite to eat or a moment of rest. He mingles with the poor, the despised, and the wrongdoers without belittling them; even public sinners, coming to their defense against mean-spirited judges. Finally, during the Passion: Maltreated by the Sanhedrin and the soldiers, belittled by Pilate and Herod, abused during the flagellation and the crowning with thorns, rejected by the leaders of the people who preferred an assassin to Him; constant abuse during the three hours He hung upon the Cross, mocked by Pharisees, priests, and people. Was there ever a king or a criminal maltreated as He was? And

He was the King of heaven and earth! And to avenge Himself, He said only this: *Father, forgive them, for they know not what they do* (Lk 23:34).

It may be possible to survey the various indications of Christ's humility and to conclude, priests especially, by a sort of rationalization that one can possess this virtue without actually renouncing the satisfaction of one's vanity, moodiness, or ambition. But is it really possible to enter the Hearts of Jesus and Mary in frequent meditation without understanding the nature of their humility and their desire for humiliations, without coming to a firm resolve to imitate them?

Even so, temptations to vanity and pride will keep coming. Often, especially in the beginning, we will give in to them imperceptibly or without thinking. Then, in all simplicity, go to Jesus with Mary and declare one's need for help and confidence. They will make clear what they would have done in our place and we will know what to do the next time. Sometimes, we are aware of what is happening, but the sinful desire is so strong we can hardly resist it. Do not rely on willpower; just think of Jesus and Mary and souls.

There will be embarrassing situations. I have been successful and people congratulate me. I cannot deny it without being insincere. We are not asked to deny what God has done for us, but to give the credit to God as Mary did in her *Magnificat*. Simply say: "Mother, I thank you and I ask your pardon. Thanks for the good you have enabled me to bring about in spite of my inadequacy. Pardon me for the other things you wish to achieve but which my weakness impedes."

At other times, there will be humiliating and annoying failures. Again, go to Jesus with your Mother. Describe your humiliation and your need for assurance. Any humiliation accepted out of love and in union with their humiliations will prepare the ground for a more substantial success. No one ever faced greater failure and humiliation than did Jesus and Mary during the Passion, and no one achieved a greater triumph than they. United to them, you will share in their triumph. A humble, Marian priest will always achieve victory, and the more humble and Marian he is, the greater will be the victory!

CHAPTER FIFTEEN

Acquiring Priestly Poverty with Mary

O Mary, Mother of the Christ-Priest, help all priests to understand the meaning and the importance of priestly poverty. A great number of them, even among those who have made a vow of poverty, fail to grasp the sense of it.

With Mary, let us reflect on the priestly poverty of Christ in order to make it our own.

In becoming a priest, Christ, *though he was rich…became poor, so that by his poverty you might become rich* (2 Cor 8:9). He did not embrace a poverty limited to necessities, i.e., one respectable in the eyes of the world, but a poverty often lacking the necessities of life—the humbling sort.

He chose a mother who was poor, whose poverty was degrading because she was of royal lineage. He was born in someone else's stable and had an animal's manger for a crib. He had to flee to Egypt with His parents, leaving all possessions behind and living from hand-to-mouth in a foreign country. During His Hidden Life, He was obliged, from an early age, to labor hard for meager remuneration.

During His Public Life, His situation was worse as He entered full-time into His priestly mission. He lived on alms. He was so indigent that He could say to the scribe who wished to follow Him everywhere: *Foxes have holes, and birds of the air have nests, but the Son of man has nowhere to lay his Head* (Mt 8:20). At the very beginning of His ministry He proclaimed poverty as the first beatitude because... *theirs is the kingdom of heaven* (Mt 5:3). He pronounced a twofold curse on the rich: *Woe to you that are rich, for you have received your consolation. Woe to you that are full now, for you shall hunger* (Lk 6:24–5). He chose to mingle with the poor and gave this preference as proof of His Messiahship (cf. Lk 7:19–22).

Poverty was a requirement for those Christ chose to assist Him in His priestly mission. He selected them from among the less prosperous and asked them to abandon the little they had. Witness the question Peter asks: *We have left everything and followed you. What then shall we have?* (Mt 19:27). It is why Jesus pointed out to the scribe who wished to follow Him everywhere, that *the foxes* and *birds* were better lodged than He was (cf. Lk 9:58). Before the young man who had observed the law could join His band of followers, he had first to *go sell what [he] owned and give the proceeds to the poor* (cf. Mk 10:17–22). When He sent His apostles on mission for the first time, *He charged them to take nothing with them except a staff* (cf. Mk 6:8). No doubt this was an arrangement peculiar to this short missionary journey, but its underlying spirit (be content with what is strictly necessary) is valid for all missionary efforts.

Such are His words and actions. But it is important to penetrate Jesus' interior, to discover the motives He had for choosing poverty for Himself and for His helpers. It is especially here that Mary is our guide. All the words and actions of Jesus flow from His love. Hence, it is certainly out of love that He chose to be poor—love for His Father and love for souls.

First of all, out of love for His Father: This poverty included the humiliations and sufferings He accepted for the glorification of His Father. It also included a complete, filial confidence that the Father would provide the necessities of life: food, clothing, etc. This confidence also glorified the Father.

Christ's poverty of hardship and humiliation was shared by Mary. It was especially on His account that she did so, particularly on the occasion of His birth and the ensuing flight into Egypt. But because Jesus chose to undergo these sufferings, she was happy to undergo them with Him, happy to glorify the Father with Him, happy to pray while facing destitution but with complete filial confidence: *Father, give us this day our daily bread* (Mt 6:11). She gladly embraced this poverty because she loved her Son and His Father in heaven. In the thanksgiving canticle she spoke to Elizabeth, she declared: *He has filled the hungry with good things, and the rich he has sent away empty* (Lk 1:53).

It was also out of love for souls that Jesus opted for this poverty. By means of it, He was able to teach them, more by example than by words, the fundamental necessity of detachment from worldly goods. When He began His sermon on the plain with the solemn declaration: *Blessed are you poor, for yours is the kingdom of God,* he added: *But woe to you that are rich, for you have received your consolation* (Lk 6:20, 24). Some time later, when the rich young man was unable to give up his wealth and He pointed out the great difficulty the rich have achieving their salvation, who would have believed this paradoxical statement had He not given an example of voluntary, strict poverty in His own life? The Gospel reports that His own disciples *were amazed at his words* (Mk 10:24). But far from altering them, He said: *Children, how hard it is to enter the kingdom of God! It is easier for a camel to go through the eye of a needle than for a rich man to enter the kingdom of God* (Mk 10:24–25). The Gospel writer said that they were exceedingly astonished and that they asked: *Then who can be saved? Jesus looked at them and declared: With men it is impossible, but not with God, for all things are possible with God* (Mk 10:26–27).

Jesus saw that it was the poor who followed Him and listened to Him with joy. He saw that it was the rich, the Pharisees, the Sadducees, the priests, and the leaders of the people who mocked Him and were bringing themselves and the nation to ruin. He foresaw that it would be the poor who would accept the Gospel most enthusiastically and who would make up the majority of the faithful. He foresaw that it would be the rich, tenaciously hoarding the wealth of the world, who would heap evils on humanity: flagrant or disguised injustices, violence and murder, the exploitation of widows, orphans, and the helpless. Plunged in physical pleasures, they would live in wanton luxury alongside people dying of hunger and cold. They would exploit the disadvantaged and make escape from this condition impossible. Because of them, whole populations would be relocated far from their homeland to work as slaves in inhuman conditions; wars would destroy the world's resources; civil wars and genocide would erupt; great numbers would leave the Church seeing it, not as their mother, but as their enemy; large groups would be intent on destroying the memory of Christ and obliterating the very idea of God, through lies and violence. All this because of inordinate attachment to worldly wealth.

What can we say about those priests who are supposed to teach the world to renounce Mammon and adore the only true God? Jesus foresaw that a great number of them would imitate His life of poverty and would teach the deprived to serve God in detachment, simplicity, and joy as true children of their heavenly Father. He also foresaw that many would renounce all material possessions by vow in order to serve Him in strict privation, and cut off from the world.

But He also foresaw that a great number of other priests would allow the love of money to set them on the road to perdition and cause the spiritual ruin of many. They stand beside the one who betrayed his Master for thirty pieces of silver and of whom it was said that *it would have been better had he never been born* (cf. Mt 26: 24). Already in the fervent, primitive communities, there were priests St. Peter had to admonish: *Tend the flock of God that is your charge…not for shameful gain, but eagerly* (1 Pet 5:2). It was especially after the Christianization of the Roman Empire—when the possibility of martyrdom ceased to motivate candidates for the priesthood, but rather the desire for temporal advantages—that many priests no longer dedicated themselves to their sacred functions but to the satisfaction of their greed and ambition. St. John Chrysostom declared them in danger of eternal damnation.

Then, during the ensuing centuries, the two great evils of simony and nepotism, rising out of priestly greed, would appear to disfigure the Church, the bride of Christ, who desired it to exist *in splendor, without spot or wrinkle or any such thing* (cf. Eph 5:27). Simony marketed priestly functions for money and great profit. Nepotism led to priestly concubinage because men entering the priesthood to enrich themselves were incapable of celibacy. In addition, the conferring of ecclesiastical benefices on men who lacked a sacerdotal vocation led to laxity and scandal in the hierarchy, the clergy, the laity and, even sometimes, especially in the monasteries. The Christian world was ripe for the Lutheran apostasy and the severance of almost half of the faithful.

The hierarchy, itself more or less contaminated, abolished these terrible abuses only in part. The enemies of the Church eliminated them by means of the confiscation and theft of a major portion of ecclesiastical holdings.

However, no one was able to eliminate from the hearts of men the three great concupiscences born of original sin, particularly the inordinate desire for worldly wealth. There continued to be priests bent on enriching themselves or promoting the material interests of their families. It was these priests that Pope Pius XI challenged in his encyclical, *Ad catholici sacerdotii*:

> Woe to the priest who…should become "greedy of filthy lucre." Woe if he join the herd of the worldly over whom the Church like the Apostle grieves: "All seek the things that are their own; not the things that are Jesus Christ's."

> Such a priest, besides failing in his vocation, would even earn the contempt of his own people.

> Greed, called by the Holy Spirit the "root of all evil," can incite to any crime.

> Even though he stops short of crime, a priest poisoned by this vice, will nevertheless, consciously or unconsciously, make common cause with the enemies of God and of the Church, and cooperate in their evil designs.

On the other hand, by sincere disinterestedness, the priest can hope to win the hearts of all.[23]

Pope Pius XII, in his turn, considered it necessary to warn his priests about temptations to greed. "Nor should you consider it sufficient to renounce earthly pleasures through chastity and to submit in generous obedience to your superiors; to these you must also unite daily a detachment of your hearts from riches and from things of earth… We strongly exhort you, dear brothers, to avoid all immoderate affection for the things of this earth, essential ones included."[24]

Thankfully, this craving for filthy lucre, condemned by the Holy Father, is not a general problem, though it does exist to some extent, in certain areas. But there are two other consequences stemming from improper attachment to material goods that many priests do not know how to guard against. These consequences, of which priests are often unaware, are capable of causing irreparable harm to souls.

The first of these is the failure to preach the social doctrine of the Church to the affluent for fear of losing some of the material resources they

---

23 *Ad catholici sacerdotii.* nn. 49–50.
24 *Menti nostrae,* n. 25.

furnish to apostolic works. Because of such neglect, the rich never hear the warnings Christ pronounced in their regard and the danger of damnation that menaces them. Because of such neglect, the poor are turned away from the Church, which seems to favor their economic oppressors, and join the ranks of atheistic, political groups. Have those priests who preached the fullness of the Gospel ever lacked the money they need for the works of their ministry? The words of Christ: *Seek first his kingdom and his righteousness, and all these things shall be yours as well* (Mt 6:33): are they not still valid?

Another baneful consequence of inordinate attachment to wealth is the need for affluence and comfort which some priests in particular localities feel are necessary for maintaining ecclesiastical dignity. Even priests who have made a vow of poverty are not sheltered from this temptation. Did the Cure of Ars lack dignity? This attitude has become a gulf separating the financially stressed from the priest. The priest who sets himself apart from ordinary people is no longer one of the people. Ordinary people keep their distance from him because he has distanced himself from them in becoming upper class. How can these souls be brought back to their Mother, the Church?

There are, of course, places where the priests live comfortably and where the faithful maintain a strong religious practice. Yes, but is this because of the priests or in spite of them? In reality, is not this active faith due to priests and teachers in religious congregations who instruct the children in accord with the Gospels? Should these priests and teachers disappear from the scene, the number of practicing faithful would be reduced by two-thirds in one or two generations.

It is not only because of the unhappy example they give, that priests should eschew an upper class life style. This manner of living is directly opposed to the Gospel. It hampers mortification, it hampers a total gift of self, it hampers conformity with Jesus Christ crucified for the salvation of the world. The life of a priest is meant to be the life of a victim as was that of Jesus. The priest who lives in affluence does not understand this truth! He understands that he is to pray and to preach, but suffering for the purpose of expiation or conversion makes no sense to him.

St. Paul set down for his beloved disciple, the young bishop Timothy, the rule for apostolic poverty: *If we have food and clothing, with these we shall be content* (1 Tim 6:8). In his exhortation to Catholic priests, Pope Pius XII expresses the same rule in other terms: "Take as your models those great saints of ancient and modern times who joined this essential detachment from earthly goods to a profound trust in Divine Providence and a most ardent priestly zeal; as a result, they produced works that are truly marvelous, confiding solely in God who, assuredly, is never found wanting in our needs. Even priests who do not make a profession of poverty by a special vow must always be guided by the love of this virtue, a love that ought to show itself in the simplicity and modesty of their manner of life, in their living quarters, and in their generosity to the poor."[25]

To master the practice of this rule, it must be observed and admired as Jesus and Mary followed it. When he does so, a priest living habitually in union with Christ and His Mother will come to understand the simplicity, the modesty, the self-sacrifice, and the total gift of self that a life of apostolic poverty will require of him. It must be pointed out that all canonized secular priests had a high regard for, and an exceptional faithfulness to, this virtue.

Many of them, as did the Cure of Ars, Abbe Chevrier, and Abbe Poppe, lived in indigence far beyond that of normal, religious poverty.

---

25 Menti nostrae, n. 25.

A priest who has learned poverty in the school of Jesus and Mary is a powerful apostle. He is strong and free because he is not preoccupied with the many exigencies of upper class life. He is infinitely happier with his impoverishment and privations than the man who tries to satisfy his every whim. He gives of himself completely; he becomes all things to all people in order to win them for Christ. He is almost indifferent to his personal needs, but he gathers large sums for his apostolic works. He knows how to guide and comfort the poor. He knows how to speak to the rich to make them aware of their duties and the dangers they face. He speaks with the frankness of an ambassador of Christ.

The poor admire such a priest and the rich respect him even though they may disagree or debate with him. He is a witness of Christ. Believers recognize him as a true disciple of Jesus. Unbelievers say that if there is an authentic Christian faith, it is the faith of that priest. It is poverty-practicing priests like these who will lead the world to Christ.

Blessed Mother, Mother of the Christ-Priest and Mother of all priests, send us a multitude of these poverty-practicing priests.

CHAPTER SIXTEEN

Acquiring Priestly Chastity with Mary

It was the distinctive glory of Mary to be both Virgin and Mother. It is the distinctive glory of the Catholic priest to be both virgin and father. Distinctive glory entails both distinctive advantages and distinctive obligations. Let us ask our Immaculate Mother to help us understand and participate in the love of Jesus and His love for chastity.

With Mary, let us reflect on the God of infinite purity, surrounded by myriads of immaculate angels, descending to earth to become a Priest serving both His Father and humankind. He needs a mother and He chooses one purer than the angels of heaven. In becoming incarnate in her and in being born of her, He not only respects her virginity by an unprecedented miracle, He also moves her to indescribable, greater holiness. He selects a virgin foster-father and a virgin precursor. His beloved disciple is also a virgin. He allowed Himself to be dubbed a banquet lover, a public disturber, a violator of the Sabbath, a blasphemer, but He never permitted the least shadow of suspicion regarding

His purity. He has given everyone, priests especially, an example that we all should follow.

Let us also contemplate and admire the purity of Mary, in whose womb He became a priest and offered Himself to His Father for the first time as expiating Victim and Adorer. It was she whom He chose to cooperate with this priesthood. Thanks to a God-given instinct, and without any prior example for doing so (in fact, a contrary ideal considered sterility in a woman to be a curse), Mary chose to remain a virgin. God, however, rendered her fecund while simultaneously preserving her virginity by a double miracle. God gave her a spouse who had also decided to live as a virgin and Jesus, before dying, confided her to a virgin apostle. It is the will of God that she help priests maintain an unsullied purity to which they are called by their sharing in Christ's priesthood.

In the company of Jesus and Mary, let us try to identify the advantages virginal purity has for the priest who is another Christ.

Even though, because of circumstances, priests of the early Church were not obliged to celibacy, still many of them decided that a complete form of chastity was more fitting for their priesthood and, on their own, followed the hope of St. Paul: *I wish that all were as I myself am* (1Cor 7:7). The Latin Church was only ratifying existing practice when it decreed that priests renounce marriage. It was a way of saying that only a virginal form of chasteness enabled a priest to ideally accomplish his obligations to God and to souls.

With regard to God, a priest is someone who, in the name of humankind, offers the Holy Trinity the homage of adoration, praise, expiation, and petition expected of him. As is the Christ-Priest, he is the Father's "special possession." As such, he should not be divided; he should be completely dedicated to the Father's business. St. Paul observed: *The unmarried man is anxious about the affairs of the Lord, how to please the Lord; but the married man is anxious about worldly affairs, how to please his wife, and his interests are divided* (1Cor 7:32–34). Pope Pius XII stated: "The more resplendent priestly chastity is, so much the more does the sacred minister become, together with Christ, 'a pure victim, a holy victim, an immaculate victim.' "[26]

The practice of chastity in its complete form is also fitting for a priest because of his obligations to the faithful, and that, for a number of reasons.

---

[26] Menti nostrae, n. 21.

First of all, in order to be free enough to give himself to the needs of the faithful without reserve. In speaking from captivity to his disciple, Timothy, now a bishop, St. Paul recommends: *Share[in] suffering as a good soldier of Christ Jesus. No soldier in service gets entangled in civilian pursuits, since his aim is to satisfy the one who enlisted him* (2 Tim 2:3–4). How can a man who has to look after the interests of his family give himself unreservedly to the needs of souls? Obliged to cater to the needs of his wife and children, how difficult it will be for him to practice and to preach as he ought, detachment from worldly wealth, to both the rich and the poor.

Secondly, the priest must preach the necessity of the virtue of purity to many people who find its observance very difficult. In preaching the obligation of chastity in accord with one's state in life, should not the priest be aware of the power given him by the practice of celibate chastity? Even without any urging on his part, his conduct preaches purity. Does not experience show that in a family where a member has become a priest or religious, other siblings find chastity easier to observe according to their state in life and to establish wholesome families?

Happily, individuals in religious life, men and women who have consecrated themselves entirely to God, assist priests by their prayers and sacrifices and their ministry to the young and the sick. And, certainly, it is easier for a celibate priest to promote vocations to the virginal life and to guide those who have entered such a life.

There is another aspect of priestly chastity to be considered. It entails sacrifice, often very difficult sacrifice, and lifelong sacrifice. Nothing expiates like sacrifice. By fidelity to his celibacy, the priest reclaims souls, lifting them from the depravity into which impurity has cast them, or winning for them the strength to resist temptations to impurity. This ministerial view of things is a support against the assaults on his purity that the priest will undergo as he seeks to preserve his purity. It involves struggles and sacrifices he can offer for preserving the purity of the souls confided to him.

In spite of the advantages afforded by priestly purity, in spite of a solemn commitment to perpetual chastity and the sublimity of a vocation superior to that of the angels, priests are still human creatures, burdened from birth with the consequences of the original sin and the sins of their ancestors.

Concupiscence is not wiped out even if it is diminished. However, there is an infallible road to victory. It is union with the Immaculate Virgin

Mary. Without a true devotion to Mary, the priest is too weak to remain standing when assaulted by violent temptations. Without Mary, he cannot win; with Mary, he cannot succumb.

For those unfamiliar with devotion to Mary, priestly chastity is an unbearable yoke, a barricade that tries to thwart nature from what it seeks to enjoy most of all. For those who know Mary well, it is a strength, an asset, an ennoblement, a genuine joy, an imitation of Christ, a call to give oneself to God and neighbor. With her, temptations are less frequent, sometimes disappearing totally and always easier to overcome.

At the present time, chastity is threatened by many dangers stemming from moral depravity in general, and frequent insidious allurements in particular instances. There is a growing excessive liberty in the relation between sexes that sometimes even intrudes upon the exercise of the ministry.

The advice of Pope Pius XII is that of Christ: "Watch and pray!"[27]

Watching and praying is more successful when done with Mary. Constant association with the All Pure One sharpens watchfulness. One acquires

---

[27] *Menti nostrae*, n. 23.

an appreciation for purity and an aversion for its opposite. Instinctively, one senses danger and avoids it. Praying is better. One recognizes that God desires to bestow on us the grace of purity through the intercession of the Immaculate Mother, and that it is thanks to her that individuals are safeguarded even in their weakest moments—some resisting hell's fiercest attacks, others regaining their purity in spite of past failures.

Other means for safeguarding purity can be pointed out. Chasteness requires the ongoing practice of mortification. The priest ought to be able to say as did that marvelous priest, St. Paul: *I pummel my body and subdue it, lest after preaching to others I myself should be disqualified* (1 Cor. 9:27).

How can anyone who offers his body every comfort and every permissible pleasure have the power to resist major, forbidden pleasures when facing strong temptations. There is a clever trap inviting the priest to pamper his body. For every deprivation imposed on nature, it seeks some compensation. To make up for the loss of the pleasures of marriage, it seeks the counterbalance of an affluent lifestyle. Mary calls her priest to become a victim with Jesus.

Chastity presumes modesty in its widest sense. Whoever surpassed the Immaculate Virgin in modesty? The Marian priest will imitate his Mother. All his conversations and mannerisms, his bearing and his eye contacts will bear the stamp of decency and indicate a son of the most chaste of virgins. Chastity is the daughter of humility. A son of Mary is marked by humility because pride and a filial devotion to the Blessed Virgin are psychologically incompatible. Humility teaches self-knowledge. Anyone aware of his weakness will stay out of temptation's way. However, corrupt nature is very cunning and suggests to a son of Mary all sorts of wily reasons urging him to approach the tree of forbidden fruit. But for a priest who regularly consults Mary about his activities and undertakes nothing without her approval, she will help him to easily discern whether these reasons are valid or merely the pretexts of passion. If his duty obliges him to become involved in a precarious matter, he will invoke her help and will undertake it in her presence, keeping in mind the intentions of God who created the human body and shared with humans his power of creating in purity and love.

When he is obliged to listen to the confession of all sorts of sins against purity, the priest will unite himself to his Immaculate Mother, and sadly regret that a temple of God has been profaned, that Jesus has been ejected from His tabernacle and replaced by the evil one, that a child of God and of Mary has been enslaved by their enemy. Instead of troubling him, that confession will bring about in him a greater love of Jesus and great compassion for the penitent.

The priest who generously accepts the constraints of celibacy will take great care to avoid undue familiarity and unbecoming conversations with even devout persons of the opposite sex. He will be particularly careful in his exchanges with unhappy women who come to him for consolation; such dealings have brought more than one priest to ruin. In necessary contacts with organizations of women, he will bear in mind the advice of Pope Pius XII: "We deem it opportune to address to you a special exhortation as regards your direction of associations and sodalities of women, that you show yourselves as becomes a priest; avoid every familiarity; when you must give your services, give them in a way that is befitting sacred ministers. Moreover, in directing these associations, let your interest be confined to the demands of the sacred ministry."[28]

---

28 Menti nostrae, n. 24.

There is another kind of temptation that can trouble a priest. It is heartache—the regret of never being able to enjoy the exclusive affection of a beloved. For a priest consecrated to Mary, this temptation is rare. His heart, completely dedicated to Jesus, to Mary, and to souls, is fully satisfied. No one loves as intensely and as genuinely as he does.

There is another challenge. Feminine influence is needed for the formation of a child and of an adult male as well. A woman is able to cultivate, sometimes even to create in men, a sense of refinement, of gentleness, of propriety, and of fidelity. That is true. But what a shared existence does for a married man, our heavenly Mother does for the priest who lives in union with her, but in a much more perfect and efficacious way. She confers on him a sense of refinement, of tact, of compassion, of forgetfulness of self, of total sacrifice that only the most perfect of mothers can bring about. The priest who has no special devotion to Mary lacks something in his nature. He is less complete, less a man, than someone who enjoys the gentle influence of the Virgin Mary.

The first Christians liked to picture the Church as a virgin mother. By means of their union with Mary, the Virgin Mother *par excellence*, the representatives of the Church will depict it in the eyes of the faithful and even in the eyes of the world, as having the qualities of virgin and mother.

CHAPTER SEVENTEEN

Acquiring Priestly Obedience with Mary

In the eyes of the world, obedience is equivalent to compulsion. Obedience as a virtue is meaningless or simply absurd. This viewpoint constantly tends to infect all of us since we are the offspring of a father who started things off with an act of disobedience. All of us have inherited that tendency.

At the present time, because of the breaking away of half of the world's Christians from the Church of Rome, and even more because of modern political and social upheavals, this rebellious spirit is stronger and more widespread than in previous ages. There is a contemporary danger that priests will assimilate this outlook. Moreover, present day ministry requires constant updating to meet new needs and circumstances and, consequently, more initiative on the part of priests than formerly. Thus, our commitment to save souls seems to warrant a watering down of the need for obedience.

But ministerial guidance does not come from the world. Catholic priesthood is a participation in the priesthood of Christ. When He came into the world Christ began an entirely new approach to ministry. In the words of St. Paul, *[Christ] became obedient unto death, even death on a cross* (Phil 2:8). If anyone understood the ministerial approach of Christ, it was Paul, the apostle *par excellence*. It was with regard to the obedience of Christ that he counseled, *Have this mind ... which was in Christ Jesus* (Phil 2:5). All through her lifetime, Our Blessed Mother meditated on Christ and His priesthood in which she would cooperate. She summed up her mission as obedience to the divine will: *Let it be to me according to your word* (Lk 1:38).

Let us enter the soul of Jesus, as Mary did, to understand His position regarding priestly obedience and to learn how to make it our own. Christ came to save a world crippled by the disobedience of Adam. Disobedience must be repaired by obedience. Hence the declaration of Christ on entering this world, *Lo, I have come to do thy will, O God* (Heb 10:7). Eve inveigled Adam into disobedience. It was fitting that the disobedience of our primal mother be repaired by the obedience of our new Mother. Hence her reply to the angel, *Let it be to me according to your word* (Lk 1:38).

Starting in the second century, the Fathers of the Church, Saints Justin and Irenaeus especially, stressed the insight that Mary's faith remedied the unbelief and disobedience of Eve. Priests can participate in the redemptive work of Christ and His Mother only by taking on their spirit of obedience.

No one can share in the redemptive mission of Christ and Mary who does not also share their spirit of obedience. People of the world and priestly confreres who share its spirit, might scoffingly remark that it is out-of-date to have scruples about obedience. It is better to be out of style with Christ and His Associate than fashionable with the enemies of Christ.

Let us examine the qualities of Christ's and Mary's obedience. Christ obeyed his Father—directly to the revelations He received from him, and indirectly to the dictates of his representatives (Joseph and Mary, as well as religious and civil authorities). Mary imitated Him. She obeyed the will of the Father, mediated to her by an angel, by Joseph, and by the prescriptions of the Law.

Like Jesus and Mary, we obey all legitimate authority, both religious and civil, because in submitting to it, we submit to God. It takes an act of faith to see God in the directives of human beings. If anyone can act out of such faith, it certainly should be the priest. The same faith, which tells him the bread he consecrates is the Body of Christ, should also tell him that the man he obeys is the representative of the Father and of Christ.

The obedience of a priest, like that of Christ and Mary, should be filial, warm-hearted and unhesitating because it is given to the heavenly Father.

It will, above all, be filial in his relationship with his bishop or his religious superiors because they share the fatherhood of God. The bishop is the father of the household of his diocesan priests. It was he who made them priests. They were ordained to be his collaborators. He gives them approval to preach, to celebrate, and to confer the sacraments in his See.

It is by means of their union with him that they receive God's blessing on their ministry. The better their union with him, the more they edify the faithful, and the more souls they save and sanctify. All this is true for vowed religious as well. For ordinary matters, they are guided by their religious superiors, but for their priesthood, the bishop is their father. It was his imposition of hands that made them priests and it is from him that they receive permission to exercise a priestly ministry. They, too, are his collaborators.

A narrow-minded and egotistical spirit, preoccupied with its own interests and those of its faction can, on occasion, cause bad feelings between the two different clergies. But a magnanimous and generous spirit, burning with the love of Christ for the salvation of the world, is happy to cooperate with all Christ's soldiers.

In religious life, the superior is the revered father of the religious priest in a different manner. Each religious congregation and each of its communities is a tightly knit family whose father is the superior. It is in obeying him with a genuine, filial disposition that its members can best promote the spiritual goals of this family and its apostolic commitments. And if this congregation is in some way consecrated to Mary, obedience to its superior is an obedience to the heavenly Mother as well, and should be earnestly filial even more.

Priestly obedience is a simple and humble obedience. Christ unhesitatingly obeyed all the representatives of His Father, even the most boorish of them. The Blessed Virgin did the same. She asked the angel in what manner the will of God would be carried out, and on receiving his explanation, she replied in all simplicity, *Let it be done to me according to your word* (Lk 1: 38). What objections she could have made! With the same trust, she arranged for the circumcision of her Child and presented Him and herself in the Temple, even though neither He nor she was bound by the relevant laws. Once a priest is aware of God's will for him, can he do other than submit to it with faith and joy?

Simplicity rejects all self-serving critiques of orders received. It does not ask, "Why me?" or "Why me and not so and so?" It renounces verbalizing every sort of criticism:

—Criticism is a way of compensating oneself for the sacrifice made in obeying a superior.

—Criticism is a way of satisfying one's vanity or pride, for to criticize is to judge, and to judge is to place oneself above others.

—Criticism is a betrayal of fairness. It disregards the fact that there are many sides to every question and that the superior is often better placed to see more of them than the subordinate. It is to take only one side into consideration. A fair-minded man cannot always say that the order given is the best course of action, but he can suspend judgment and maintain silence.

—Criticism is the smothering of the spirit of obedience in oneself and in others.

—Criticism destroys the unity needed among those fighting for Christ against His enemies who are united under Satan. It is not these enemies who are the greatest danger. That comes from priests who criticize and who cultivate a spirit of criticism.

—Criticism kills enthusiasm and, without enthusiasm, nothing great is ever accomplished.

An obedience marked by simplicity does not inhibit respectful observations made to authority in the hope of clarifying a situation about which one is puzzled. But the last word remains with authority.

The obedience of a priest should be total, like that of Christ and Mary. Jesus faithfully carried out, to the smallest detail, everything His Father willed. In recording the crucifixion of his Master, St. John reports: *Jesus knowing that all was now finished, said (to fulfill the scripture), 'I thirst'* (Jn 19:28). Inspired by the example of their Chief, priests will follow the law of love and humbly carry out all the directives of even those superiors with whom they disagree.

They will even anticipate them, without obvious fawning.

Far from inhibiting initiatives in the ministry, total obedience will foster them. It is the hope of their superiors that priests will obey, not as machines, but as intelligent persons, carrying out their orders with personal know-how and goodwill. Initiatives contrary to the directives of superiors are not responsible ones. Saints who were responsible for important undertakings that revolutionized the religious world were all men of scrupulous obedience.

In his exhortation to the clergy, *Menti nostrae*, Pope Pius XII says: "We are far from holding that the apostolate must not be in keeping with the reality of modern life and that projects adapted to the needs of our time should not be promoted. But since the whole apostolate carried on by the Church is by its essence under the control of the hierarchy, new forms must not be introduced save with the Bishop's approval... Let everyone be persuaded of this: that it is necessary to follow the will of God and not that of the world, and to regulate the activity of the apostolate according to the directives of the Hierarchy, and not according to personal opinions. It is a vain illusion to think oneself able to hide one's own inner poverty and still cooperate effectively in spreading the Kingdom of God by novelties in one's method of action."[29]

For centuries (and for how many yet to come?) all the heresies and schisms that have torn the Church apart, and caused the loss of many of its members, were born of the disobedience of priests who wished to change it to fit their personal ideas.

O Jesus, you declared: *O God, I come to do your will,* (Heb 10:7), and you saved the world. Your Mother said: *I am the handmaid of the Lord, let it be to me according to your word* (Lk 1:38), and she became your Associate in the work of redemption. I am your priest. I come to do your will. I am the son of your handmaid; let it be done to me according to your will! With you and with her I will save souls.

---

[29] Menti nostrae, nn. 119–120.

CHAPTER EIGHTEEN

Glorifying God with Mary

On entering this world, Christ declared: *Sacrifices and offerings thou hast not desired, but a body hast thou prepared for me; in burnt offerings and sin offerings thou hast taken no pleasure. Then I said, 'Lo, I have come to do thy will, O God'* (Heb 10:5–7). The primary goal of Christ-Priest is the glorification of His Father. That should be the primary goal of every priest as well.

Unfortunately, there are many priests who, in practice, if not in theory, manifest more interest in their ministerial functions than in the glorification of God. Ministry has a stronger appeal to the senses and to the imagination than praise and atonements offered to God.

What does priestly ministry gain from such a reversal of values? Is apostolic work that ignores the interests of God in favor of human beings more helpful for souls? Is it not rather the satisfaction of a need for activity or for accomplishment or for ascendancy? Does it not result in pique or apathy when obstacles or failure are faced? Are not God's glory, his love, and his desire to save all men and women the most powerful motives for working until completely exhausted for the salvation of souls? The declaration of Joan of Arc is forever valid: "O God, it is you I serve above all!"

Let us study our Model. Having come into the world to offer His Father a fitting sacrifice, He glorified him in all that He did. He told the Jews, *I honor my Father and you dishonor Him* (Jn 8:49). He glorified him by continually doing his will. *I always do what is pleasing to [my Father]* (Jn 8:29). *My food is to do the will of him who sent me* (Jn 4:34).

The will of the Father sometimes entailed painful sacrifice; He came to save the entire world but had to limit His ministry *to the lost sheep of the house of Israel* (cf. Mt 15:24). To carry out the work of His Father, He had to inflict great suffering on His Mother (cf. Lk 2:34–5). The cup of suffering His Father asked Him to accept made Him recoil in dread, yet He accepted it. *Father… not my will but thine be done* (Lk 22:42). His final word, like His first word, concerned the will of God. Observing that all the Scriptures had been carried out, He declared, *It is finished* (Jn 19:30), and concluded, *Father, into thy hands I commit my spirit* (Lk 23:46).

He tried to help His disciples know and appreciate the Father. How lovingly He spoke

to them about him. He urged them to surrender
themselves completely to the Father who watches
over the flowers of the field and the birds of the air
and especially over his children (cf. Mt 6:25–34).
He taught them to pray to the Father, instructing
them to request, first of all, his glorification,
the accomplishment of his will and the coming
of his Kingdom on earth (cf. Mt 6:7–15). He
counseled them to be true worshipers of His Father,
worshipping Him in spirit and in truth (cf. Jn 4:23–
24).

It was to His priests, the apostles, that He
spoke with a special tenderness. Because they had
faithfully remained with Him, He said the Father
had a special love for them. He prayed that the
Father protect them from the world, sanctify them
in the truth and give them a share in His own
reward. On the morning of His Resurrection, He
told Mary Magdalen, *"Go to my brethren and say to
them, I am ascending to my Father and to your Father,
to my God and your God"* (Jn 20:17).

These are only a few indications of Jesus'
sentiments in regard to His Father. The Gospels
record numerous passages in which He speaks about
him explicitly. But it can be said that the entire
contents of all four Gospels furnish evidence of His
filial regard for him, because when He preached to

the crowds or healed the sick, it was to make loving children of the Father from those who did not know him, or who had offended him and were on the way to spiritual ruin.

It is this filial relationship of Christ with the Father that priests should endeavor to imitate. Hence, they should continually dwell on it in their meditations and try to emulate it during each day. Evidently to have a clear idea of Jesus' infinitely loving regard for His Father, it is necessary to penetrate the very Heart of Jesus. Who can deny that it is under the guidance of Mary that one most easily enters this Heart? It is in the company of our Mother that one comes to have an incomparably better insight into the Christ-Priest's love for the Father, the love that should be the priest's as well.

The more we become aware of her filial love for the heavenly Father, the more effective will Mary's help be in this loving effort. She possessed this filial love even before becoming Christ's Mother. From the moment she knew God—no doubt from the moment of her Immaculate Conception—she saw many indications of the Creator's love for her and she responded to this infinite love of the Father with an unconditional filial gratitude and love.

As she became aware of other human beings and that, without any merit on her part, she was immeasurably more favored than they—that she was a very privileged daughter of the Father—her filial love grew day by day. At the same time, she could not help but see that the worship people offered the Father was merely material and external. By her love, she spontaneously tried to compensate for what was lacking in theirs.

Gabriel announces that she has been chosen to be the Mother of the Son of God. She and the Father will have the same Son. From that moment on, how much more intense must have been her need to love the Father and to take on her Son's filial regard for him. Jesus spent His first thirty years of life in close company with Joseph, and especially with Mary.

What was this intimate relationship like? We do not know. But for certain, they frequently exchanged views about the Father, about his infinite love for humankind and especially for the three of them. Christ's filial love for His Father was absorbed by His Mother as fully as a mere creature possibly could. And along with this love, she took on His dominant desire that the Father's name be glorified, that his Kingdom be established, and that his will be carried out on earth as it is in heaven.

During the day, while Jesus worked with His foster-father, Mary lovingly meditated on these points. For her, as for Jesus, the Father was everything. She knew that her Son was going to be immolated for the glory of the Father and all his children. And as terrifying as this prospect was, she gladly accepted the fact that, along with her Son, she too would be immolated in her heart for the same purpose.

Once we come to realize the unique filial regard Mary had for the Father, even before Jesus began His public life, we will more easily understand along with her, the things Jesus told His disciples about the Father. Priests will come to appreciate the Christ-Priest's filial love for the Father; they will admire it, cherish it, and ask Jesus and Mary to share it with them.

How can this filial stance of Jesus become a reality in daily life? Even for the priest most deeply immersed in the demands of the ministry, opportunities will not be lacking. Too often it is the failure to endeavor achieving Christ's special filial love that is the cause of a priest's failure to notice these moments of grace and to profit from them. Many of them can be found in the Liturgy.

During the celebration of the Sacrifice of the Mass, recall the intentions the Redeemer and the Coredemptrix had when this Sacrifice was offered on Calvary. A Victim of infinite value was presented to God, giving him more glory than all the crimes that humankind had taken from him. The celebrant can unite himself as a victim with the divine Victim. Many prayers of the Mass express these sentiments. In the opening prayers: "Glory to God in the highest." In the preparation of gifts and the Preface: "be pleased with the sacrifice we offer you…for the praise and glory of his name…to praise you day by day for the marvels of your wisdom and power…to receive the praise of the Church on earth." In the Eucharistic prayer: "we come to you with praise… we offer to you, God of glory and majesty…all glory and honor is yours." In the Communion rite: "Jesus taught us to call God our Father…pray for the coming of the kingdom… hallowed be thy name."

In the prayers of the breviary, references to the glory of God are frequent:

"Glory to the Father… Your name is worthy of all praise… I will praise you all my life… May our lives proclaim your goodness… Praise and exalt him forever… Let them praise his name with dancing." Every Lord's Prayer, every doxology, the *Te Deum*, the canticles at morning prayer and evening prayer, phrases in psalm after psalm, etc. Take notice of these references and try to pray them with Mary in the same way she prayed the psalms long ago in Nazareth, in the spirit of her *Magnificat*. Further on, in Part Three, we will explain how to assist at the Holy Sacrifice and how to recite the Divine Office in union with her.

In addition to these official prayers, there are opportunities to glorify God in many private devotions. In the most common of these, the Rosary, the glory of God is referred to at the beginning and end of every decade and also in the Lord's Prayer and the Glory to the Father. The Blessed William Joseph Chaminade recommended to his disciples that, at the beginning of each hour of the day and each time they awaken at night, they offer this little prayer: "May the Father and the Son and the Holy Spirit be glorified in all places through the Immaculate Virgin Mary."

CHAPTER NINETEEN

Mary Stimulates a Yearning for the Salvation of souls

It was on behalf of men and their salvation that He descended from heaven. The Son of God became man not only for the glory of God but also for our salvation. In reality, this twofold purpose fuses into a single goal:

Jesus making expiation in our place restores God's glory and simultaneously presents to His Father, as worshipers in spirit and in truth, those who were in rebellion since the time of Adam. Even Christ's name declares His mission: Jesus-Savior (God saves). While He lived to glorify the Father, He also breathed, worked, suffered, and died to redeem all men and women. This should be the goal of every priest as well. The priest who cannot claim this goal as His own is not an authentic priest of Christ.

It is in reflecting on the zeal for souls that engrossed Jesus, that our hearts will become enlivened by the same eagerness. Here, as always, it is in the company of Mary and under her guidance that this reflection on Christ the Savior should take place. Reprising with her the meditations on priestly self-denial described in chapter thirteen we will see how, from the first moment of His entry into this world until his final crying out on the Cross, He sought to serve and not to be served. It was a martyrdom lasting thirty-three years, culminating in the agony of the crucifixion.

His service was our salvation. He did not end it with His Death and Resurrection. He wanted its continuation until the end of time. To this end, He established His Church, instituted the priesthood, gave us the Sacraments and the re-presentation of His Sacrifice on the Cross. Of all His actions on earth, He arranged for the re-presentation of only one: the Calvary Sacrifice that saved us and, in its re-presentation, continually makes application of its saving grace. The repetition of this Sacrifice is not limited to a service performed once a year on an altar atop a Judean hill, but uninterruptedly, thousands of times a day, everywhere on earth. It takes place before a group of people who do not seem to realize what is going on, and by straitened priests who are distracted and in a hurry, and seemingly unaware of the significance of their action.

With Mary, we will stand in awe before these amazing arrangements, invented out of Christ's love, for saving souls from eternal damnation.

With her, we will ask Him to ignite in our hearts some of the fire that burned in His. However, we must not be content to admire externals. Once more, we should enter into the Heart of Jesus, as Mary did, to learn the motives that prompted Him to save us at such a price.

The Son of God ... loved me and gave himself for me (Gal 2:20). St. Paul said it is this love that explains His extravagant zeal for our salvation. He saw God loving his creatures with an infinite love, creating them out of nothing because of this love, giving them a share in divine life because of this love, and because of this love, always ready to pardon them if only they accept his love. What incomprehensible folly that he should love a creature so wicked, so ungrateful, so arrogant. The Son-of-God-become-man shared this incomprehensible folly. It explains why He pursued the most hardened and repugnant sinners, never giving Himself a moment's rest, spending Himself for them to the last drop of His Blood, submitting Himself, the infinitely lovable one, to indescribable tortures.

With Mary, let us sound the depths of Her Son's love and mercy. With her and with her help, let us seek to transfer into our hearts some of His passion for saving souls. A priest becomes a priest to assist in the work of salvation. If, while insisting he loves

Christ, he does not yearn for the salvation of these souls so excessively loved by Him, is he not a living lie?

While trying, in company with my Mother, to participate in Christ's infinite love for souls, I will become aware that I am also sharing in the posture of her Immaculate Heart, a Heart indescribably sorrowful and merciful. Jesus' love for souls is completely shared by her. Like her Son, she loves souls with the Father's love. She also loves them for personal reasons—because she sacrificed her Son for them; because by adoption they are her children, other Christs, other children of the Father; because it is her mission to rescue them from Satan so that they may live the life of her First Born. Recall how ardently Monica yearned for the conversion of her son, Augustine. The ardent yearning of Mary for the salvation of her straying children in danger of eternal damnation is immeasurably greater. Can I truly claim to be her favored son if I do not seek the salvation of these children with all the ardor I can muster?

The gate is wide and the way is easy that leads to destruction, and those who enter by it are many (Mt 7:13). There are many souls, too numerous to count, facing a future in the depths of hell, who should be rescued by those who have received an apostolic mission. A priest is one called to this task. Jesus and Mary are counting on him. Can any one of them fail to be driven by a yearning and an all-out effort to save souls?

When I am tempted to commit some fault or just an imperfection, or when I pass up a chance to be generous in some way, these souls are begging me, "Have pity! Save me from hell!" I must remember the agonizing plea of Christ on the Cross, "I thirst. I thirst for souls!" I must not forget the tears of my Mother, standing before her dying Son, weeping for this Son and weeping for those other children of hers I am not seeking to save for her.

Jesus! Mary! Souls! Souls! Let this plea for the salvation of souls haunt me day and night and compel me to exercise my priesthood to its full extent.

CHAPTER TWENTY

Mary and Priestly Responsibilities

In his encyclical on the Mystical Body of Christ, Pope Pius XII made a statement that challenges priests to take stock of themselves and perhaps even makes some of them uneasy. Speaking of the cooperation that they should offer Christ in the work of saving and sanctifying men and women, he wrote:

> Because Christ the Head holds such an eminent position, one must not think that He does not require the help of the Body. What Paul said of the human organism is to be applied likewise to the Mystical Body. *The head [cannot say] to the feet I have no need of you* (1 Cor. 12:21). It is manifestly clear that the faithful need the help of the Divine Redeemer, for He has said, *[Without] me you can do nothing* (Jn 15:5), and according to the Apostle every advance of this Mystical Body towards its perfection derives from Christ the Head. Yet this, also, must be held, marvelous though it may seem: Christ has need of His members. That is not because He is indigent and weak, but rather because He

has so willed it for the greater glory of His Spotless Spouse. Dying on the Cross, He left to His Church the immense treasury of the Redemption, towards which she contributed nothing. But when those graces come to be distributed, not only does He share this work of sanctification with His Church, but He wills that in some way it be due to her action. This is a deep mystery, and an inexhaustible subject of meditation, that the salvation of many depends on the prayers and voluntary penances…and cooperation of pastors of souls which they must offer to our Divine Savior.[30]

What the Holy Father said about Christ can also be applied, the needed adjustments having been made, to Mary, His Associate in the work of our salvation. To rescue souls from Satan, to sanctify her children and bring them to resemble Jesus, Mary needs priests. That is not because she is indigent or weak, for she is the Distributrix of all graces, but because it is the will of God. Because he deals with human beings as intelligent and free creatures, he asks that they cooperate with Christ and with His Mother in the work of Redemption.

---

30 Mystici corporis Christi, n. 44.

A deep mystery indeed, and one upon which we cannot meditate enough. The salvation of a multitude of souls for whom Christ shed His Blood, and Mary, her tears, depends on the prayers and mortifications and collaboration that priests must offer to the Redeemer and His Coredemptrix. Meditate on this. Meditate on it ceaselessly. The salvation of a myriad of souls is worth the effort.

Every Christian should be an apostle because every Christian is baptized into another Christ come among us for our salvation. But Christ has charged some of His disciples with a special, collaborative mission in the work of Redemption. *When [Jesus] saw the crowds, he had compassion for them, because they were harassed and helpless, like sheep without a shepherd. Then he said to his disciples, 'The harvest is plentiful, but the laborers are few; pray therefore the Lord of the harvest to send out laborers into his harvest'* (Mt 9:36–37).

In speaking of the conversion of pagans, St. Paul quotes the prophet Joel, *And it shall come to pass that all who call upon the name of the Lord shall be delivered* (Joel 2:32). And he then remarks, *But how are men to call upon him in whom they have not believed? And how are they to believe in him of whom they have never heard? And how are they to hear without a preacher? And how can men preach unless they are sent? As it is written, 'How beautiful are the feet of those who preach the good news!'* (Rom 10:14–15).

Without a doubt, *God ... desires all men to be saved* (1 Tim 2:4). He offers every soul sufficient grace to attain eternal life. *Many will come from east and west and sit at table with Abraham, Isaac, and Jacob* (Mt 8:11). God will not damn anyone because of some fault on the part of an undependable apostle. Anyone who is lost is lost by his own fault. Yet, it is also true that he would have received much more help for attaining heaven, if the individual God called to bring him that help, had been faithful to his mission. resume

Every individual, even if a heretic or a pagan in good faith will be taken by God to live with the saints in heaven if he has lived in accord with his conscience objectively correct. But how many of the human family who are deprived of the Faith and the help of the Sacraments live in accord with their conscience? Speaking about the pagans of his time, St. Paul speaks about sins against nature, and hence against conscience, committed by the majority of them. Is the situation of modern pagans any different? How many Christians, strengthened by the grace of Baptism and the light of the Faith, can keep themselves in the state of grace when they are dispersed among unbelievers and deprived of the

Sacraments of Penance and the Eucharist for long periods of time?

In actuality, we all have need of such a superabundance of spiritual helps brought to us by those called to do so that, where they are lacking, even many Catholics cannot live according to their conscience. Depending on whether or not those called to apostolic mission are faithful or unfaithful to their vocation, a multitude of souls will be saved or lost. This is indeed a "deep mystery," one on which we can never meditate enough.

Priestly responsibilities can be considered from another point of view.

Many members of the faithful, whose faith and love are feeble, still act and react out of fear of eternal punishment. What should really motivate them is the glory of God and love for Our Lord. One so dedicated praises God much more, has a greater sense of fulfillment, and contributes more effectively to the work of saving souls than a thousand mediocre souls, even though they are in the state of grace. The efforts of priests should not be merely to save souls from sin but to help the faithful attain this degree of holiness.

The history of the Church bears witness to outstanding success in the ministry on the part of those called to it. During the first three centuries after the death of Christ, the Christian faith spread out with astonishing rapidity in spite of bloody persecutions. Had it continued to grow at the same rate, the bulk of the world's population would now be bending the knee before Jesus. But at the present time, only one fifth of these people profess the Catholic Faith. Two thirds are pagan or Islamic. What happened? During those first three centuries, most Christians, both priests and laity, were animated by their call to be witnesses for Christ. But as the fourth century began, many of the clergy began to be more concerned about themselves than about Christ and their missionary mandate. Still, each time an especially responsive person took this mandate seriously and devoted himself or herself completely to it, countless numbers were converted or led to great holiness. Who can say how many more blessed there are in heaven or how many blessed love God more deeply because of the work of St. Francis of Assisi, St. Dominic, St. Teresa, or of so many others? We can answer, "Millions!" because the number includes not just those directly touched by the actions of these Saints, but also their natural or spiritual descendants.

On the other hand, if gifted and called individuals who were fully responsive to their graces accomplished such marvels, there were other gifted and called individuals who were unfaithful to their call and who caused the defection of many. Arius, Luther, Calvin were all clergymen who received exceptional abilities from God for influencing others.

Imagine the immense amount of good they could have accomplished had they responded to what God had in mind! Imagine the great mischief they caused, and the unfortunate situation that still exists thanks to Luther and Calvin, because they were unfaithful to their call. Similarly among those who have caused great harm in our day, we must mention Renan, Combes, and Stalin—all former seminarians!—and Hitler's inspiration, Nietzsche, who was the son and grandson of exemplary Lutheran pastors and an aspirant to Christian ministry. A gifted and chosen individual cannot be neutral. He either accomplishes much good or incalculable harm.

All the same it was not only the spirit of pride and rebellion on the part of certain individuals called to the priesthood that deprived the Church of so many of its members. This loss is also attributable to hosts of others who believed, or still like to believe, they are true to their priestly obligations.

On the Cross, Christ destroyed the foundation of the devil's power. On the eve of His passion, He declared, *Now shall the ruler of this world be cast out!* (Jn 12:31). *He has no power over me!* (Jn 14:30).

By His victory over the devil, Jesus has made us invincible. *Be of good cheer, I have overcome the world* (Jn 16:33).

The true priest of Christ has a crushing superiority over the devotees of the devil. He has at his disposal an unlimited supernatural force—the power of the sacraments and the backing of the entire Church. The devotees of the devil are limited to natural skills. But even from a natural point of view, the true priest has received a basic formation superior to most of them, and a specialized training longer and more intense than theirs. He preaches a message of truth, while theirs is made up of lies and falsehoods. His teaching addresses the noblest and most fundamental aspirations of mankind while theirs purveys unreliable, physical pleasures. Unencumbered by the demands of a secular occupation, the true priest can devote all his time to the salvation of souls while the evil efforts of those others are limited to the free time their occupational careers and family involvements allow.

How is it then, that in the eyes of the masses, the cause of Christ seems vanquished? Why does the Church mourn the loss of so many of her children? Why do so many of those who call themselves Christians think and act like pagans? There are a certain number of priests (happily on the increase) who give themselves to their ministry without reserve. But, unfortunately, there are also a large number of other priests who are simply content to chat with and administer the sacraments to those who come their way. Should they not be pursuing souls, exhausting themselves and sacrificing themselves after the example of Christ and His apostles?

The Popes continually offer important teachings to the faithful regarding their social justice obligations. How are these teachings to be passed on to the workaday faithful? By the priests, evidently. Why is it then that so many working class people and company executives are ignorant of the Church's social justice teachings? Because of this, many individuals who were once loyal to the Church are now separated from her and even see her as an enemy. What a terrible neglect on the part of many priests! It amounts to a betrayal of Christ and His message! This neglected responsibility is a mystery to be pondered.

I am a priest. I was called to the priesthood by Christ and His Mother. In God's plan, a certain number of souls are to be saved, thanks to my ministry. How Many? I do not know. Perhaps a very large number.

Francis of Assisi, Francis Xavier, Dominic, Ignatius, Canisius, Teresa and Thérèse, and many others have contributed to the salvation and sanctification of millions! But they were Saints! True, but they did not start out as saints. Before their change of heart, many of the greatest missionaries of the Church seem to have committed more sins than I have.

When Francis, the playboy of Assisi, decided to imitate to the letter, the poverty of Jesus; when Ignatius, the elegant soldier whose morals were those of his peers, resolved to serve no other King but Jesus; when Francis Xavier, who constantly dreamed of glory, honor, and advancements, came to understand there was no advantage in winning the world if you lost your soul in doing so; when the young Peter Canisius, who believed himself to be the most accomplished citizen of Nijmegen, where his father was burgomaster, made a retreat and became a Jesuit; when Teresa of Avila decided to give up her lengthy drawing room visits and converse only with God; when they made these decisions, did they foresee that their about-face would people heaven with countless souls?

Can I live with the thought that, because of my lack of zeal, a single soul might suffer terrible despair for all eternity, curse God and the Virgin Mary, and curse me who could have saved him? But I am not called to save a single soul. No, I am called to save the many souls, perhaps a host of them that God has confided to me.

Should I be content to carry out the strict obligations of the priesthood in an acceptable manner, I might keep intact an average Christian practice on the part of most of the faithful I serve, and I might even absolve a dozen sinners who have been away from the sacraments for a long period of time. People would honor me as a good priest. But had I been determined to be a *saintly* priest I would have converted a thousand or more. What, then, will happen to the nine hundred eighty-eight I could have converted? The world will see what I have done and praise me for it. It will not see what I could have done and ought to have done. But Christ, who died for those nine hundred eighty-eight and called me to win them over, will see it. The Blessed Virgin, who became their Mother while undergoing her sufferings on Calvary, will see it. I will have disappointed Them because I found it too difficult to forget my own benefit and to expend myself unreservedly for the salvation of souls. They never hesitated to undergo the most terrible of martyrdoms for me.

If I carry out those priestly duties that moralists consider obligatory under pain of sin, I surely will not be condemned. The infinitely merciful Heart of Jesus will forgive me for my watered-down zeal and will grant me heavenly bliss. Yet, it is also true that there will be souls, perhaps a great number of them, who will not be saved as a result of my chicken-heartedness. Can I find peace in this egotistical consolation: "As long as I get to heaven, too bad for those who are damned! They had sufficient grace for attaining salvation!" I could also add: "And too bad for their heavenly Father and for Christ and their Mother!"

There are legal obligations for which one has to answer in a court of justice. There are other obligations beyond the purview of the court for which one is no less responsible. These can flow from a tacit agreement between friends, from gratitude, from fellowship, from love, from mutual understanding. For a high-minded person, these obligations are also binding even more than the others. If I am a Catholic, if I am a priest, I am so because of the prayers, sacrifices and efforts of many individuals, known and unknown. I have received so much! Ought I not give in return?

Jesus has been especially generous towards me. He not only called me to the Catholic Faith; He called me to the priesthood. I realize He has need of me and that He counts upon my assistance for the realization of His redemptive work on earth. Mary, too, has been especially generous towards me. She, the Distributrix of all graces, has heaped preferential graces upon me. She too is counting on my help. Moreover, I am consecrated to her. By a solemn declaration, I have given her the right to direct me, not only in the accomplishment of my strict obligations, but also in regard to all that I have, all that I am, all that I do, and all that I am going to have, or be, or do. Can I now ungratefully and egotistically betray the trust of those who have loved me so much and given me so much? I owe it to myself as a matter of honor; I owe it to Jesus, I owe it to Mary, and I owe it to souls to spend myself to exhaustion in the service of Christ and Mary and souls.

O Jesus, in the Garden of Olives, you were gripped by discouragement and terror; you were sorrowful unto death and you prayed: *Father, if it be possible, let this cup pass from me; nevertheless, not as I will but as thou wilt* (Mt 26:39). What a terrible vision of the future it must have been that drew this prayer from You when, only a short time before on leaving the Cenacle, You told your apostles, *I do as the Father has commanded me, so that the world may know that I love the Father. Rise, let us go hence* (Jn 14:31). What premonition overpowered You at that moment? The terrible sufferings and death that awaited You? No doubt, in part they did.

But also, and even more so, it was the vision of sins You had to expiate. It was the picture of all the sins of the world, from the sin of Adam to that of the last person on the earth. These most horrible, hateful, and repulsive sins which outraged the infinite holiness of Your Father weighed upon You and made of You an object of loathing.

But was there not another vision that you wished to wipe out at all costs? It is the vision of all the souls that may be eternally lost in spite of all You have done and suffered for them. A Christian mother prays for years and suffers great torment to save a son in danger of perdition. How crushed would this poor mother be if, in spite of her tears, prayers and sacrifices, he seemed to die impenitent! And You, Jesus, can see all souls—and among them, the vast number who will be lost in spite of Your prayers and sufferings and the blood You shed for them. You love the most wicked of them more than Monica ever loved Augustine.

You see priests among the lost. You instituted the priesthood to confer on special friends the task of continuing Your redemptive work to help You save souls. Many of them responded to your call. These are the saintly priests who dedicated and sacrificed themselves completely and helped You bring thousands and thousands of souls to the Father. But at this Gethsemane moment, You also see other priests to whom You lovingly extended Your call and of whom it could be said, as it was said of the one about to betray you, it were better had they never been born. The vision shows You all the souls that will be led astray by their perverse teaching and scandalous example. And You see still other priests saved because of fidelity to their required obligations—but slothful and egotistical— who, out of indifference and foot-dragging, made no effort to pull back from the precipice those You intended them to lead to the Father, but who are now lost.

O my Mother, you whom Jesus wished to associate in all His privileges, in all His mysteries, in all His joys and sufferings, you must have shared His Gethsemane agony in some mysterious way. You who are going to offer up your Son for the salvation of souls whose Mother you are to become, you are made aware at this moment that, for many of them, your sacrifice will be for nothing—they will be stillborn—you will never see them beside you in heaven. In part, this will be because of the weakness or negligence of a number of your beloved priests.

O Jesus! O Mary! In Your agony You suffered much for my sins! But I do hope that You did not suffer because of souls lost due to my negligence! I beseech You to help me do whatever it takes to save the souls You have confided to me. May not one of them be lost!

But to save all of them, what prayers, what sacrifices and what efforts must I make? How will I know whether I have done enough? Oh, I see!

When God calls someone to a special task, He also grants him all the graces necessary for carrying it out properly. He made us *competent to be ministers of a new covenant* (2 Cor 3:6). To save all the souls You have confided to me, I have only to be faithful to the graces given me—and to all those graces, give me the strength and will to do so.

No doubt, it will happen more than once that I will fail to properly evaluate what is going on, or that I will hesitate to carry out one of Your wishes. When that happens, Jesus, I will come to You in the company of my Mother, with my grief and my trust. I know You will accept this as an expiation for the benefit of souls. If I am able, I will try to do more. To the extent that my generosity has been lacking, I will search with Your Mother to find ways of making it greater. In that way, my fault will be a "happy fault" for You, for souls, and for me. In the name of Your immaculate and sorrowful Mother give me the ability to say as You did before leaving earthly life, *Holy Father…I have guarded all those you have given me and none of them is lost because of me* (Jn 17:11–12).

CHAPTER TWENTY-ONE

Acquiring Priestly Charity with Mary

The most essential manifestation of charity is Christian zeal. But not all zeal is born of charity. The priest must penetrate the charity of Christ in order to be familiar with the zeal that should animate him. Supernatural charity consists in loving Christ in our neighbor and in loving him as Christ loves him. Jesus Himself teaches us this. He said, in speaking of the last judgment, *whatever you did ... or failed to do ... regarding the least of my brethren, that you did ... or failed to do ... to me* (cf. Mt 25:40–5; Acts 9:4).

To acquire the charity of the Christ-Priest, one must meditate on His words, actions, and attitudes, noting how each of them flows from the infinite love of His Heart. As always, these meditations should be made in union with Mary. Who ever penetrated the Heart of Jesus as she did? Who ever took into his heart the dispositions of the Heart of Jesus better than she did?

In situations that call for the practice of charity one must ask, or better, one must ask her, "Mother, what would Jesus do were He in my place?"

It is also important to meditate on the charity of Mary. The Scriptures record a number of instances of it in her life: her *fiat* at the Annunciation, her visit to Elizabeth, Mary and the shepherds, Mary and the Magi, Mary with Simeon and Anna, Mary at Cana, Mary on Calvary, Mary in the Cenacle. Sometimes, perhaps, Mary's charity sways us more than that of Jesus. Mary is both Virgin and Mother. She was created to carry out a unique mission of love. Jesus is the limitlessly loving Savior, but He is also a legislator and judge who sometimes must castigate the Pharisees or harshly reprimand disciples slow to believe. In assimilating the charity of Mary, we can more easily comprehend the charity of Jesus since it was from Him that she received whatever of this virtue she possessed. Her charity is a finite participation in the infinite charity of Her Son.

Mary teaches us how to be a *mother* to souls. She is a Mother who understands sorrow and can empathize with it perfectly, who consoles and encourages, who sacrifices herself without holding back, who finds it natural to live only for her children, giving them herself and all that she has without looking for any return. The Church is a mother and priests represent this mother-Church in the eyes of the faithful. Mary can instill in their hearts her own maternal love.

For Jesus—love, His special Commandment— is the *greatest Commandment!* It is the new Commandment He came to give us and the one by which we will be judged. He wants us to love each other as He loves us. It is the way we— priests especially—will be seen as His disciples (cf. Mt 22:37; Mk 12:23–33; Jn 13:34, 15:12). We all know in theory that charity is the priority commandment of Christ. But in practice, is it really so for priests? For some, the most important quality is the ability to organize. For others it is the ability to govern, or eloquence, or knowledge, or know-how, or fund-raising. Are these the qualities Christ used to win over disciples? He did it by *doing good* (Acts 10:38), by lovingly *giving himself for us* (Gal 2:20). St. Vincent de Paul exercised a widespread influence in seventeenth century France. He did not achieve it by his knowledge or eloquence, but by his inexhaustible charity. If Francis Xavier converted a myriad of pagans in India and the East, it was not his eloquence or even his miracles that won them over, but his tireless and unselfish dedication. Francis de Sales reestablished the Catholic Faith by his optimistic and light-hearted charity, in regions earlier lost to reformers.

A priest of average ability but marked by irrepressible charity can, by a simple word, get a positive response from the faithful and compel the respect and trust of unbelievers. Christ is love. A priest exemplifies Christ, not by reasoning, but by becoming the love that is Christ. Contact with such love breaks down all resistance. The shortest and most certain path to becoming the love that is Christ is to meditate on that love with His Mother who, herself, is this perfect love.

Jesus' love was *unselfish*. He helped and worked miracles even for those He knew would not remain faithful. In the desert, He fed His miraculous bread to people He knew would abandon Him the very next day in Capernaum. When Mary asked Him to provide wine for the wedding guests at Cana, He did it to save the hosts from embarrassment and to keep the party from being spoiled without any assurance the revelers would draw spiritual profit from it. When a priest gives someone an alms or a service, he should do it to serve Jesus and not to buy the right to give a little sermon.

Note well the unselfish character of the charity of Jesus and Mary. Most people love other people because of some good they see in them or hope to see in them. It is for the personal satisfaction it gives them and so it is basically egotistical. Or they do it because they see qualities similar to their own, giving them opportunity to improve their qualities, or because they see qualities different than their own that make up for what they lack. Jesus and Mary love us not because of any good they find in us but because of the good they wish to give us in whom there is nothing but sin and the tendency to sin. It is with this love that priests should love others. When they see only sin and evil habits in individuals, Jesus and Mary will teach them how to love these people and how to help them live more like Jesus.

It is in exerting zeal, the most perfect manifestation of charity, that unselfishness is critical.

Zeal is the most honorable or the most dangerous of qualities depending on whether or not it is exercised with unselfishness. Acting with zeal affords many satisfactions—gratification from achievement, gratification from influencing others, from mastery, from accomplishment, from honors, from praise, from the success of one's ideas or methods, from gratitude, from admiration, or even from financial remuneration. It is difficult to avoid taking great pleasure in some of these satisfactions and thereby courting great risk. The danger of losing his own soul in seeking the salvation of other souls is not a chimera for a priest. If he is not watchful, he can be serving himself when he imagines he is serving God and so lose much of the spiritual merit that would come to him for the work to which he devoted himself. That would be a personal loss, but it would also render him incapable of doing for souls two-thirds of the good he could do for them had he acted unselfishly.

What is the safeguard? It is a loving look towards Jesus and Mary. What were They looking for in their long martyrdom for us? They wanted only the glorification of the Father and our salvation. That should suffice for us as well.

Jesus' charity is *universal*. He loved everyone and died for everyone. He did not exclude obstinate sinners, hypocritical Pharisees, or His calumniators and tormentors from His love. Mary shared this attitude. She loved everyone and considered herself Mother of everyone. She sees every person as purchased by the Blood of her Son and seeks to have them live the life of her Firstborn. If a priest loves only those who agree with him and regards non-practicing Catholics—especially scandalous ones—heretics, Masons, and Communists not worth worrying about, does he have true Christian charity? Does he really possess Jesus and Mary's love?

It is especially in the exercise of zeal, that one's charity should manifest its universality. Every priest should have a special interest in the ministry assigned to him; that is the will of God. But it is not God's will that he be unconcerned about other ministries. From a natural point of view, indifference to ministerial groups or apostolic efforts different from his is a manifestation of narrow-mindedness. From a supernatural point of view it is a preoccupation with his own glory instead of God's glory.

Sometimes under the pretext of zeal or *esprit de corps*, or team spirit, a priest gives in to shabby, shameful temptations. For example: jealousy because of another's success, along with a need to belittle or disparage his work; or joy because of another's failure, especially if he feels that another's success is superior to his own. Another trap is indifference to the good or evil that occurs outside one's limited, at times decidedly limited field of responsibility. The Church is *catholic*. Anyone, whose exercise of zeal is not universal, lacks the spirit of the *Catholic* Church. Jesus died for all men and women. Mary is the Mother of all God's children. They seek the salvation of all souls. Whoever loves Jesus and Mary rejoices at any advance of the cause of Christ, no matter by whom or in what way it comes about. He deeply regrets the loss of souls, no matter what the cause. He is happy to lend his assistance to other apostles even if they alone will get the credit. As long as Christ is known and loved, and as long as Mary can win Him many disciples, our own glory does not count.

The charity of Jesus is *patient, deferential, and winsome*. Jesus could say to His apostles, *I am gentle and lowly in heart, and you will find rest for your souls* (Mt 11:29). He was forbearing and patient with the impatient crowds that harassed Him at all hours. He was forbearing and patient with His apostles, who, in spite of all His efforts to instruct them, remained deaf to His words and who, even after three years of training, manifested misunderstanding and many shortcomings. He was patient with His enemies, tolerantly reasoning with them despite their bad faith, and praying for them on the Cross while they jeered at and blasphemed him. St. Paul entreated the Corinthians by *the meekness and gentleness of Christ* not to force him to act otherwise (2 Cor 10:1). Jesus rebuked two of His closest disciples who were angry with the inhospitable Samaritans and wanted *to bid fire come down on them from heaven and consume them.* He said: *You do not know what you are saying. The Son of Man has not come to condemn men but to save them* (cf. Lk 9:51–56).

And as to Mary, is it possible to picture her other than meek, humble, patient, and winsome towards all? Remaining close to her, a priest takes on, little by little, her maternal gentleness and her unfailing patience towards everyone. All the faithful are her children and she knows that they cannot be saved or led to holiness except by a God-like patience. She knows that a harsh word or a sharp remark spoken out of impatience can destroy confidence and close the heart. She knows how many individuals have abandoned the practice of the Faith because of the impatience or harshness of a priest who is supposed to be another Christ. And she also knows the thousands of souls who have been won over to God by priests who have welcomed them with the gentleness and patience of her Son. If you are easily irritated or prone to impatience, make frequent meditations with Mary on the gentleness, humility, and patience of Jesus. If the irritation seems too much for you, quickly turn to Mary and say, "Mother, this is your child. Help me love him with your love!"

The charity of Jesus is *forgiving*. No one ever suffered greater injustice than He. Did He ever hold a grudge? He spoke His first words on the Cross on behalf of His enemies. *Father, forgive them; for they know not what they do* (Lk 23:34). He pardoned His brutal executioners as well as the hypocritical Pharisees and malevolent priests who reveled in mocking His confidence in the Father and the good He did in His lifetime. He forgave the crowds who, only five days prior, had acclaimed Him, but were now voicing the jeers of their leaders. Aside from the glory of His Father, His mission had no other goal than the forgiveness of sinful men and women, including His enemies.

Jesus is the model we are to imitate. He particularly desires that we forgive as He did. In teaching His disciples to pray, He included in the Our Father, the obligation to forgive offenses against us, as a condition for receiving forgiveness for our own sins. He emphasized this condition in

His parable about the servant who refused to remit the debt of a fellow servant.

Jesus wants us to forgive our offenders from the bottom of our heart and not just act impassively towards them. We should replace bitter and vengeful feelings with a prayer for them. He insisted on this. *But I say to you that hear, love your enemies, do good to those who hate you, bless those who curse you, pray for those who abuse you…so that you may be sons of your Father who is in heaven* (Lk 6:27–8; Mt 5:44–5).

Bitter feelings can often entrench themselves in the heart of a priest. He can be the victim, or imagine himself as the victim of deceitful enemies of the Faith, of lax Christians annoyed at being recalled to their duties, of arrogant faithful who think they know more than he does, of fellow priests who find fault with him, of superiors who do not understand him. Jesus had to put up with all that and much worse. Yet He said, *Father, forgive them; for they know not what they do* (Lk 23: 34).

O Mary, at the Cross, you certainly prayed along with your Son, "Father, forgive them; for they know not what they do." You have forgiven us all for we have all crucified your Son. Teach your children, especially your priests, how to forgive from the bottom of their hearts those they have never hurt.

There are many other qualities that mark the charity of Jesus. St. Paul, who extols this virtue very highly, enumerates its principal characteristics,

Love is patient and kind, love is not jealous or boastful; it is not arrogant or rude. Love does not insist on its own way; it is not irritable or resentful; it does not rejoice at wrong, but rejoices in the right. Love bears all things, believes all things, hopes all things, endures all things (1 Cor 13:4–7).

This enumeration is not an exhaustive list of all the qualities of Christ's charity. If we set ourselves to study in loving meditation the charity of Jesus and Mary, we will slowly come to the point in our relationships with others, where we interiorly feel what Jesus Christ and His Mother Mary feel. Our charity will resemble theirs even if their names are not invoked.

CHAPTER TWENTY-TWO

Mary Imbues the Priest with Invincible Confidence

The priest's mission seems hopelessly difficult. Has the world ever been as depraved as it is today? Have Satan's cohorts ever been as numerous, as fierce, as cunning? Has the army of Christ ever been weaker compared to these powerful forces? A priest will lose confidence if he thinks about the enemy in comparison to himself. But it is Christ he should think about. Christ has given him His mission as the Father gave Christ His mission (cf. Jn 20:21). He is an ambassador of Christ (cf. 2 Cor 5:20). Christ has declared, and He cannot be wrong, *When I am lifted up from the earth, I will draw all men to myself* (Jn 12:32). *Now shall the ruler of this world be cast out* (Jn 12:31). *Be of good cheer, I have overcome the world* (Jn 16:33).

Acting in the name of the Son of God, he is all-powerful with the power of God. Acting in his own name he is as weak as the weakest of men. He is feeble when depending on himself alone; he is unbeatable when he acts with Jesus. When he acts in the name of Jesus, his very weakness is an encouragement. Recall how the great Apostle boasted of his weakness so that the power of Christ could be shown through him (cf. 2 Cor 12:9). *Consider your call, brethren; not many of you were wise according to worldly standards, not many were powerful, not many were of noble birth; but God chose what is foolish in the world to shame the wise, God chose what is weak in the world to shame the strong. God chose what is low and despised in the world, even things that are not, to bring to nothing things that are, so that no human being might boast in the presence of God* (1 Cor 1:26–9).

Jesus bequeathed His Mother to all men and women to bolster their confidence. It was to John, the priest, representing all priests, that she was directly given. Perhaps this was for the purpose of bolstering the confidence of priests most of all.

In his exhortation, *Menti nostrae*, Pope Pius XII counseled priests, "When you meet very serious difficulties in the path of holiness and the exercise of your ministry, turn your eyes and your mind trustfully to her who is the Mother of the Eternal Priest and therefore the loving Mother of all Catholic priests."[31] He made reference to some recent, wonderful events witnessed by many priests when they consecrated their flock to the Immaculate Heart of Mary and then concluded, "To the Beloved

---

31 Menti nostrae, n. 141.

Mother of God, Mediatrix of heavenly graces, We entrust the priests of the whole world in order that, through her intercession, God will vouchsafe a generous outpouring of the Spirit which will move all ministers of the altar to holiness and, through their ministry, will spiritually renew the face of the earth."[32]

If priests follow the intent of the Holy Father and personally consecrate themselves to the Immaculate Virgin Mary, they will find in this total gift of themselves to Mary, a special motivation for complete confidence. Consider the following: they belong entirely to Mary; their efforts are her efforts; their success is her success; their failures are her failures if, following her desires, they should fail.

Mary wills their success:

— because it gives glory to God;

— because it promotes the mission of her Son;

— because it benefits the Church, born of Him and her on Calvary;

— because it benefits her children to whom she gave birth at the cost of great suffering and of whom she seeks to make other Christs;

---

32 Menti nostrae, n. 143.

— because she desires this success more than they do: a sweeping, boundless success.

This success is certainly within her power. Is she not the Woman destined to crush the head of the serpent? Is she not the Distributrix of all graces of conversion and sanctification intended for all those confided to her priests? Before undertaking any endeavor, they should consult her to be sure it is her endeavor and not theirs. Then they can move ahead with complete confidence keeping in mind, as much as possible, that they are acting in her name. Without Mary they cannot succeed; with Mary they cannot fail!

PART III

PERFORMING PRIESTLY MINISTRY WITH MARY

NOTE: *The tenets of faith are the same for everyone. They are fairly well understood by any person having simple notions of theology and asceticism. But the practice of faith is another matter. It is based on the acquisition of habits developed over a long period of time even for the most responsive. Then too it has to take into account differences in temperament, preferences, education, and experience. Hence the following caution:*

Of the suggestions that now will be offered, follow only those that are suitable for you at the present time. Perhaps in two or five or ten years, on rereading these pages, you will better understand and more easily be able to practice what now seems unsuitable for you.

CHAPTER TWENTY-THREE

Celebrating Mass with Mary

The Sacrifice of the Cross was the crowning action of the priesthood of Christ. The Mass of a priest, the re-presentation of the Sacrifice of the Cross, is the paramount action of the priesthood.

A single drop of Christ's Blood is sufficient to purify the entire world of all its sins. If the hundred thousand Masses celebrated every day were celebrated fervently, how quickly the world would be transformed. Mary can help a priest celebrate his Masses in the most worshipful way possible.

First of all, note the relationship between Mary and the Sacrifice of the Mass.

1. The Sacrifice of the Mass is essentially the same as the Sacrifice of Calvary. Now it was the will of God that Mary, informally but really, have a part in the Sacrifice of Calvary. She was to be the Coredemptrix assisting her Son. As such, she had to offer the heavenly Father the same victim he did— her very own Son. She did this by abandoning her maternal rights over Him and by uniting her will and her sufferings to Christ's will and sufferings. His intentions were her intentions. Thus, by divine

decree, Mary's oblation was an integral part of the Sacrifice on Calvary.

A Mass from which Mary is excluded is not the comprehensive Sacrifice of Calvary. It is a truncated sacrifice. Let not men separate what God has joined together! Mary, in heaven, retains the dispositions she had on Calvary. She remains united to her Son being offered on the altar. She wills the sacrifice of this Victim whose Mother she is forever. She wills it for the same intentions as her Son.

2. The Sacrifice of the Mass *applies the merits* gained by the Sacrifice of the Cross. All merits were gained once and for all on Calvary. The Sacrifice of the Mass does not gain new merits. It brings to particular souls, according to the Council of Trent, what Calvary gained for all souls in general. Now Mary is the Distributrix of all graces merited on Calvary. That means that she has a special role to play in the Mass, the rite in which this distribution is carried out profusely.

3. *The first beneficiary of Calvary's graces was Mary herself.* It was in virtue of the foreseen death of her Son that Mary was preserved from original sin in her Immaculate Conception and enriched with the fullness of grace. At the present time, the application of the merits of Calvary to Mary

does not consist in an increase of her graces, but in an escalation of her glory and her influence in the world. In the Eucharistic liturgy of Trent at the end of the Offertory in the *Suscipe,* the Most Holy Trinity is asked "to accept this oblation which we offer *in honor of blessed Mary, ever virgin.*" Every Mass contributes to the extension of Mary's reign on earth.

4. On Calvary, Mary, in giving birth to us, brought us divine life. In every Mass, this *grace of divine and Marian filiation increases within us.*

5. It is noteworthy that during the Sacrifice of Calvary, *Jesus confided Mary* to a priest and in his person, to all Christ's priests. In the Sacrifice of the Mass, this special relationship between Mary and priests is strengthened and their closeness to her is steadily intensified.

Practical exercises:

The more a priest, by means of earnest meditation, becomes aware of the close relationship between Mary and his Mass, the more easily he will see and understand the union that ought to exist between himself and her during the celebration of this holy mystery.

Before celebrating the Eucharist, a priest should ask Mary to unite him to Jesus, Priest and Victim, so that he will be sure to offer it for the intentions of Jesus as well as his own. Routine can make one insensitive to the most sublime of divine mysteries. This is not the case with Mary. For her, every Mass is a reliving of the drama of Calvary with its unspeakable suffering and infinite love. It is the crowning point of Jesus' life of prayer, work, and suffering. It is the fulfillment of the promises voiced by Gabriel in her home at Nazareth. It is the solemn moment of earth and heaven's conciliation, of the Father's perfect glorification, and his adoption of sinners as his children. It is the hour at which, by her union with Jesus, she contributed to the fulfillment of His mysteries and gave birth to us as other sons and daughters. When, before celebrating Mass, he asks Mary to unite himself with Jesus, she will not bring all these details to the priest's attention, but she will sweep away all base and selfish momentary preoccupations, allowing him to celebrate with devotion the Liturgy that has gone on for twenty centuries.

While celebrating the Eucharist, the thought of Mary will come to mind from time to time to a priest who is well aware of the identity of the Mass with Christ's Sacrifice on Calvary, and the part Mary played in it. He should not try *to imagine the Blessed Virgin standing next to him* or to make any special effort to pay attention to her at the cost of turning his thoughts away from Jesus. Mary wants to help him fix his thoughts on Jesus and not distract him from that. St. John on Calvary fixed his gaze on Jesus, yet he was aware of her presence beside him, an awareness that bolstered his consciousness and love of Jesus.

At certain moments during the Mass, the thought of Mary will surface in the mind of the priest when her name is mentioned: During the *Confiteor* when he seeks through her intercession the purity befitting the oblation of a Victim infinitely pure; during the *Credo* when her role in the Incarnation and Redemption is recalled; in the *Eucharistic Prayer* when she is honored along with all the holy ones of heaven; at the *sign of peace* to invoke the Queen of Peace for the peace the world cannot give.

There are other times during the Mass when thoughts of her could fittingly come to mind: At the Offertory to foster all the sincerity and devotion possible for preparing the gifts in accord with the intent of the prayers; at the Lord's Last Supper, words to heighten awareness of sacerdotal identification with Jesus, Priest and Victim, offering Himself for the glory of the Father and the salvation of the world, while the Blessed Virgin offers Him to the heavenly Father for the same intentions. The priest does not see her nor does he imagine her presence, but she is there as a motherly influence, helping him to enter more fully into this mystery of love and redemption over which he presides. In the Communion rite, the priest becomes one with Jesus, and Jesus becomes one with the priest. Christ said, *He who eats my flesh and drinks my blood abides in me and I in him* (Jn 6: 56). The priest eats Him as host, i.e., as victim. It is as a victim then that He abides in the priest; it is a grace that Mary had. *It is not I who live; it is Christ who lives in me* (Gal 2: 20). May he grant the priest His three great loves: love for the Father, love for His Mother, and love for souls.

It is possible to make much more of this union with Mary during the Mass, but this requires an extremely close union with her, one that comes after a long period of interaction with her. During each of the prayers of the Liturgy one can cast a *spiritual glance* at her, as it were, in order to make her understanding of the prayer one's own and so purify and intensify one's understanding of it. This will be more fully explained in the following chapter. In this way, union with Mary during the Mass is constant and, by that fact, union with Christ is more constant as well. The priest becomes more assiduous, more focused, and more loving. But remember the caution: follow only what is suitable for you at the present time.

After celebrating the Eucharist it would be appropriate for the priest to add the *Magnificat* to his customary prayers. That was the canticle Mary originally prayed when Christ dwelt within her as He now does in the priest.

Thus, with her, he can give thanks, express his love, offer himself once more as victim, and request graces for himself and others. He should particularly express gratitude that he has one who is so pure, so humble, so noble for his Mother; one who formerly suffered much but now is so honored, the one by whom he and all priests are favored sons.

During the day the priest will have opportunities to live out the Mass.

When called upon to make a sacrifice, he should recall his morning Mass and his identification there with Christ as victim, and ask the Blessed Virgin to obtain for him the strength to always be both priest and host, like her Son and with her Son.

CHAPTER TWENTY-FOUR

Praying the Divine Office with Mary

The Divine Office is the sacerdotal prayer *par excellence*. The Church enjoins its recitation on priests.

Obedient to this duty, the priest continues down through the course of ages, to do that which Christ Himself had done, who *in the days of his earthly life, with a loud cry and tears, offered up prayers and supplications...and was heard because of his reverent submission* (Heb 5:7). This prayer has, without doubt, a singular efficacy because it is done in the name of Christ, 'through our Lord Jesus Christ,' who is our Mediator with the Father, presenting to him incessantly, His own satisfaction, His merits, and the infinite price of His Blood. It is truly 'the voice of Christ,' who 'prays for us as our Priest, prays among us as our Head.' By the same token, it is always 'the voice of the Church,' which takes up the sentiments and desires of all the faithful who unite their voices to the prayers and faith of the priest in praising Jesus Christ and, through Him, render thanks to the Eternal Father, obtaining from him the assistance which they need in their lives every day and every hour.

The canonical hours should be recited 'worthily, attentively, and with devotion,' as we are reminded at the beginning of the Office. The priest ought to pray with the same intention as the Redeemer. So that his voice is, as it were, the voice of the Lord who, by means of the priest, continues to implore from the most merciful Father the benefits of the Redemption; it is the very voice of the Lord with which the armies of angels and saints in heaven and of all the faithful on earth are associated, to render due glory to God; it is the voice of Christ our Advocate by which we receive the immense treasures of His merits.[33]

To pray the Divine Office *worthily, attentively, and with devotion,* Mary's assistance will be most efficacious. The psalms express various ideas and attitudes of a soul towards God—praise, admiration, thanksgiving, regret, confidence, supplication. By uniting himself to Mary while praying them, a priest will find these sentiments becoming more intense and refined. His faith becomes more unshakable,

---

33 Pope Pius XII, *Menti nostrae*, ns. 39–41.

his hope firmer, his love more ardent, his hatred for sin more sincere. He praises God more fervently, thanks him more spontaneously, and entreats him more confidently. The spirit of Mary becomes, as it were, that of the priest.

This sort of spiritual transfusion from the heart of Mary into the heart of the priest happens every time he unites himself to her in any prayer. It happens during the prayers of the Mass as was pointed out in the previous chapter. It happens during personal, private prayers as will be explained in the following chapter. But it happens most naturally while praying the psalms. The psalms were the customary prayers of devout Jews; they were also the customary prayers of Mary. She prayed them with Jesus and Joseph when they were with her. She prayed them by herself when they were at work. In reciting these prayers with her, the priest prays these sacred texts as she did long ago with a fervor beyond description. The priest will take on some of this fervor.

Some of the psalms make reference to the life and triumphs and sorrows of the Messiah. Who can say what feelings flooded the soul of Mary, exciting her, cheering her, overpowering her as she pronounced these inspired words? The life of Saint Catherine of Siena records that one day, Jesus appeared to her and she began to pray the Office with him. When they came to the *Gloria Patri*, instead of saying; *and to the Son*, she nodded to Jesus and said: *and to You*. What a delight this was for the virgin of Siena. How much greater was the joy of the Virgin of Nazareth when praying these psalms with her Son wherein He is mentioned, not just in a doxology, but in the entire text! These are some examples:

> *The Lord's revelation to my Master:*
> *'Sit on my right:*
> *your foes I will put beneath your feet.'*

This Master, whom she refers to as *my* Master and whom God invites to sit at his right while His enemies prostrate themselves at His feet, is her very own Child now praying beside her.

> *Before the dawn I begot you.*

He is the Son she conceived while remaining a virgin.

> *My heart overflows with noble words. To the king I*
> *must speak the song I have made.*
>
> …
>
> *You are the fairest of the children of men*
> *and graciousness is poured upon your lips;*
> *because God has blessed you for evermore.*

Happy mother! He has looked with favor on his lowly servant.

My God, my God, why have you forsaken me?
You are far from my plea and the cry of my distress.
                    …
But I am a worm and no man,
scorned by men, despised by the people.
                    …
Yes, it was you who took me from the womb,
entrusted me to my mother's breast.
To you I was committed from my birth,
from my mother's womb you have been my God.

O Simeon, you predicted: This child is set for the fall and rising of many in Israel and for a sign that is spoken against, and that a sword will pierce through your own soul as well. Behold, I am the handmaid of the Lord; let it be done to me according to your word.

In addition to psalms that are clearly Messianic, there are many others in which Mary no doubt saw allusions to her Son. The authors of the New Testament saw signs of Christ and His Kingdom in a great many texts of the Old Testament that did not mention the Messiah directly. It was the same with Mary. For her, the king prefigured her Son, and the enemies of the king prefigured Satan and his cohorts. Israel prefigured the community of believers. Condemnations meant for the enemies of David foreshadowed those meant for the enemies of Christ, understood not as spirits, but as their evil schemes. Their defeat and the victory of the king forecast their ultimate submission to her Son.

Occasionally a priest should take as the subject of his meditations the thoughts and feelings Jesus and Mary had when, in their home or in the Nazareth synagogue, they recited the songs attributed to their ancestor, David. The thoughts and feelings of Mary were those of her Son. Praying with her at His side, the priest will more easily and more deeply enter into the thoughts and feelings of Jesus. Thus, his praying of the Divine Office will become truly priestly because he will be praying with the mind and heart of the Christ-Priest.

CHAPTER TWENTY-FIVE

Praying Personal Prayers with Mary

In addition to the Canonical Hours, Pope Pius XII recommends that a priest offer personal prayers. Because of the requirements of the ministry, most priests cannot spread out the breviary prayers over the day as do contemplative religious. They risk spending long prayer-less periods in routine activities. To hallow these activities, as it were, a priest needs to bathe them in his personal prayers. Experience has shown that for priests who cannot find time for prayers other than those of the breviary, the Divine Office and even the celebration of the Mass become dull formulas and vacuous rites.

As for vocal prayers, Pius XII pointed out that "piety and the true and ardent spirit of prayer are to be valued more than a mere multiplicity of prayers."[34] The spirit of prayer is made up of two elements: a clear realization of personal inability to fulfill one's obligations and an unshakable confidence in the help of an all-powerful God. To be a "spirit" these two elements must operate as a habit, a habit that instinctively activates when there is a need for it.

---

34 Pope Pius XII, Menti nostrae, n. 48.

This "piety and this true and ardent spirit of prayer" come spontaneously to a priest closely united to Mary. She makes him realize the need he has for heavenly help if he is to lead to God those confided to him. It is because he sensed his debility that he came to Her who can and will obtain for him the help he needs. Moreover, because his close union with Mary engenders in him an ardent desire to save the souls who count on him, he is even more aware of his need for help. Priests who do not appreciate devotion to Mary have little appreciation for humility, the realization that without God's help they are powerless. And *vice versa*, those lacking humility have no devotion to her, or merely a required one.

Another point to note is that Mary gives a priest complete assurance of success. The priest is well aware of Mary's unbounded desire to save and to sanctify the souls to whom she gave birth on Calvary and for whom Jesus shed His Blood. He also knows that Jesus never refuses His Mother anything. And so, simply by asking her to carry out her maternal intentions for souls, he is absolutely sure of success. His close union with Mary instinctively leads him to have recourse to her maternal heart in every phase of his ministry. Always aware of his inability to respond fully to the needs of souls and knowing that Mary is at his side, he instinctively turns to her and, by a word or just a glance, asks her assistance.

Among the many traditional prayers to the Blessed Virgin, Pius XII in his apostolic exhortation recommended the recitation of the Rosary in particular.[35] For centuries this prayer has been considered by the faithful and by the Sovereign Pontiffs to be the preeminent prayer of the apostolate. Since Leo XIII, in particular, the Popes have unfailingly endorsed this prayer for all the major needs of the Church. The Blessed Virgin herself has requested its recitation in several of her apparitions, notably at Fatima where, when asked to reveal her name, the beautiful Lady replied, "I am the Queen of the Rosary." If this prayer is so favored in Catholic circles, should priests not also cherish it as their ministerial prayer? Saint Clement Marie Hofbauer said that when he was called to the bedside of a dying sinner, he was sure of that soul's repentance if he had time to pray the Rosary before his arrival. Priests who are not noted for their holiness, but who have faith in Mary and zeal for souls, have made similar claims. Since the Rosary is divided into decades, it is possible for a priest to pray one or two of them when he has a little free

---

35 Pope Pius XII, Menti nostrae, n. 49.

time. And if he cannot pray ten *Aves*, he can at least pray one.

There are other prayers to the Blessed Virgin a priest may offer even when occupied with the absorbing duties of his ministry. One of the most efficacious is often a short one. It is the invocation of the name of Mary or its equivalent: "My Mother!" As we explained in chapter ten, such a prayer is capable of expressing a multitude of sentiments. It can mean: "Have pity on me!" or "Help me!" or "Thank you!" or "Forgive me!" or "Teach me!" or "Change me!" Because of the variety of meanings it can have, it does not become tedious by repetition, as ordinary formula prayers do. It can be prayed anywhere—before, after, or during the most absorbing occupations or animated conversations. It can be offered during the languor or suffering of sickness, while working or at rest, while eating, when wakened at night, etc. There are few ways as adept for creating and maintaining a life of close union with our heavenly Mother, for expressing confidence, love, and joy, as this repetition of the words "Mary!" or "Mother!"

While Jesus traveled through Galilee or Judea, preaching, healing, transforming souls, or contending with Pharisees, Mary, in her home at Nazareth, continually prayed for the success of her Son. By means of her prayers, no matter how physically distant from Him she might be she was working with Him for the salvation of the world. In our day, she has many imitators, other virgins who by their prayers and sacrifices assist the present-day successors of Christ in their missionary efforts. These are the religious, contemplatives especially, of various orders and congregations. In their ministry, especially on particularly important occasions—preaching a mission or a retreat, launching an apostolic undertaking, at Easter time or on special feast days—priests should mobilize as many of these religious as they can to serve as their collaborators. It is their mission to pray for priests. They are happy when priests seek their collaboration permitting them to carry out their providential call. It stimulates and nurtures their zeal. Many of them have a sacerdotal spirit greater than many priests. In any case, their collaboration multiplies a priest's ministry by a hundred or a thousand percent.

Priests should also have recourse to the sick they know. Mary loves these individuals with a special love because of their greater resemblance to her crucified and redeeming Son. The offering up of their prayers and sufferings will also make a valuable difference in a priest's efforts. In addition, by seeking their assistance and making them aware of their role in the Mystical Body of Christ, priests will help them to be more spiritual-minded, more resigned, and more like Christ.

CHAPTER TWENTY-SIX

Administering the Sacraments with Mary – General Observations

1. According to St. Thomas Aquinas, it is principally from the Passion of Christ that the Sacraments draw their power, and by the reception of the Sacraments, we are, in a way, linked to the Passion. Through her involvement in the Passion of Christ, Mary *fittingly* merited for us what Christ merited for us *by right*. Consequently, the grace of the Sacraments comes to us principally from Christ and in a secondary way from Mary. In the administration of the Sacraments, a priest is the instrument of Christ first of all but, in an adapted way, of Mary as well. Awareness of this unique involvement of Mary can amplify a priest's fervor when administering these sacred rites.

2. The purpose of the Sacraments is to confer or to foster supernatural life, i.e., the life of Christ. The giving and nurturing of life are maternal functions and the giving and nurturing of Christ-life is Mary's mission. Priests, then, are the helpers of the Blessed Virgin when they administer the Sacraments. They should keep this in mind; otherwise, in carrying out these rites, they risk becoming functionaries repeating mere formulas and empty gestures.

3. By means of the different ceremonies and prayers of the ritual, the Church expresses its intentions and thoughts relative to the bestowal of Christ-life to the soul. It is important that the priest reflect on them in order to assimilate them and to tie them together with the intentions and thoughts of Mary in the way suggested for the psalms. United with Mary, the priest will be more fully aware of bestowing Jesus.

With the help of these observations, a priest can more easily find ways in which he can perform this part of his priestly ministry with greater faith and love, and increased profit for souls. What follows are some brief suggestions for each of the Sacraments.

Baptism

This Sacrament marks the spiritual birth of a soul to the status of a child of God and Mary. Thanks to the action of the priest, Mary has given the world another Christ. If it is customary or if circumstances permit, the Baptismal ceremony should be followed by a consecration of the infant to Mary. Suggest to the godparents or to one of the parents that when the child reaches the age of understanding, they inform him of his special allegiance to his spiritual Mother, the very Mother of Jesus, and that if he loves her faithfully, he will one day join her in heaven. If such a formal consecration is not possible, the priest can still, by a simple pious intention, entrust the child to his heavenly Mother.

Confirmation

The Holy Spirit made holy the soul of the Blessed Virgin from the first moment of her existence, overshadowed her to make her the Mother of God, and descended on her and all those praying in the Cenacle with her for ten days, transforming them all. This same Holy Spirit will now descend on these baptized adolescents to make of them witnesses and apostles of Christ. How ardently must Mary desire that they receive the divine Paraclete in great readiness and truly become genuine disciples of her Son, ready to acknowledge Him in all the challenges of life! In preparing these young people for the reception of this Sacrament, the priest should bring these thoughts to their attention and exhort them to pray to the Blessed Virgin at the present moment and throughout their lives, especially when they have an opportunity to be Christ's witnesses.

The Eucharist

The Eucharist is the real Body and Blood of Christ: the Jesus Mary brought into the world and offered for adoration to the shepherds and the Magi, and to Simeon and Anna. The priest is emulating Mary when he offers this Sacred Body to the faithful. May every priest remember this when he distributes the Eucharist! And may every priest teach the faithful how to prepare for receiving the Eucharist with Mary, and how to make their thanksgiving with her, by asking her to lend them her Heart, and by asking Jesus to transfer from His Heart to theirs, the love He bears for His Mother.

Reconciliation

It is especially important that the priest be aware of his union with Mary because it is here that he will help her restore Christ-life to souls and help it grow. It is also in the administration of this Sacrament that the priest risks becoming a mere functionary, bored by the monotony and seeming sterility of this task—listening to lists of sins, imposing penances, pronouncing the formula of absolution, urging the sinner to avoid evil and remain in a state befitting reception of the Eucharist. He must keep in mind that he is Jesus—the Jesus who comes to save sinners, the Jesus who mingled with tax collectors, prodigal sons, prostitutes and thieves. With Mary, who is full of mercy and goodness and the refuge of sinners, he can come to share the attitude of Christ toward the evildoers who came to him.

Always mindful of Mary beside him, the priest should listen to these accounts of sins asking God to pardon them, while at the same time wondering what questions he should ask and what advice he should give. Before responding to the penitent, he will ask Mary to help him find the words that will enlighten, hit home, and bring the penitent to true sorrow and a firm intention to change. Then he will not fail to mention to the sinner that, in the case of certain temptations which keep recurring and which seem too powerful to resist, he can surmount them, if he invokes the help of Mary Immaculate before whom all the powers of hell tremble in helplessness. She will bring him the help of an all-powerful God. In the past, many others as weak as he experienced this help, and experienced it daily. To penitents who keep their Christ-life intact, he will explain how their heavenly Mother wishes to assist them in perfecting this life. This is treated in the following chapter.

When confessions are over, he will ask Mary to reinforce or to repair what he tried to do for her sons and daughters.

Anointing of the Sick

By means of this Sacrament, the priest advances the mission of Mary in regard to a sick person, who may be in danger of dying, by intensifying in him the Christ-life we are all meant to live in heaven. How earnestly the Mother of God desires the successful conferring of this Sacrament! It means that all that Jesus and Mary have done and suffered for souls was not in vain. The priest should try to arouse and strengthen in the sick who receive it, sentiments of sorrow for past failures, confidence in God for the present, and abandonment to His love for the future. Let the priest bear in mind that Mary, his Mother, is always ready to bring forward and deepen these sentiments in souls, especially in those who may soon be on their way to eternity. For them, the memory of what they did in the past to honor her will be a consolation. Each time they prayed the Rosary, they asked her fifty times to pray for them at the hour of their death.

When this Sacrament is conferred on a person very close to death, the priest may be confronted with special challenges. It may be that of a person of weak faith and practice who has committed sin after sin. In his youth he no doubt did say some "Hail Marys" and attend some services honoring Mary. He may have ignored her for a long time, but she has never forgotten him. Reminding him of his youthful regard for Mary, and bringing to his attention words he often heard about her goodness toward sinners may arouse confidence in her. Anyone who surrenders himself to Mary is on the path to heaven.

It may be the case of one who has never honored Mary. Let the priest then speak of her and her goodness, explaining her title, "Refuge of Sinners," and describe the suffering she endured with her Son on Calvary to win his eternal salvation. Or it may be the case of a completely obstinate sinner. Let the priest then have recourse to means other priests have found effective—the recitation of the Rosary and recourse to the Miraculous Medal with the prayer: "O Mary conceived without sin, pray for us who have recourse to thee."

Holy Orders

Recall what was said of Mary in chapters two, three, four and five:

"Mother of Christ-Priest, and in a special way, Mother of every priest"; "Mary, Associate of Christ-

Priest, whose vicars are the priests"; "Mary, Symbol and Mother of the Church, whose agents are the priests"; "Similarities and parallels between Mary and the priests."

Matrimony

The purpose of this Sacrament is to bless the union of spouses in the procreation of offspring who are meant for eternal life, as intended. How can Mary be unconcerned about these children of God who will be her children, other Christs, as well?

The priest should make these marital partners aware of the similarities they have with Mary's situation. They must learn, as she did, how to love one another with a deep, unselfish, and generous love; how to support each other in difficulties; how to share joys and sorrows, trials and consolations.

They can obtain from her the grace to keep their marriage vows unblemished. If, at times, conjugal fidelity calls for heroism, she can win them this heroism in the same way she wins it for the unmarried, or for those who have decided not to marry, who have recourse to the Virgin of virgins.

They should ask her to bless the children they will bring into the world; they should offer these little ones to her before they are born; they should consecrate them to her at the time of their Baptism. They should seek her help in learning how to raise their children and they should teach them, by word and example, how to have a real filial piety towards their heavenly Mother. They should love their offspring as Mary loved her Son. It is not their own gratification that should motivate them in this, but the love of God and the good of the children. Should God call one or more of them to His special service, they should be happy to encourage a positive response.

CHAPTER TWENTY-SEVEN

Practicing Spiritual Direction with Mary

The mission of a priest includes more than helping the faithful to enter the state of grace and to sustain it. Every Christian is another Christ. A priest should help this Christian grow in the divine life until he has come *to mature manhood, to the measure of the stature of the fullness of Christ* (Eph 4:13). But to confer the life of Christ and to model on Him the upbringing of those possessing it: is that not the mission of her who originally gave Christ to the world and was charged with His upbringing? Is it not also the mission of her who is the Mother of every member of the Mystical Body because she is the Mother of its Head?

To carry out her mission, Mary needs priests, but they have an even greater need of her. It is the realization that they are cooperating with her in nurturing Christ in the faithful, that gives them insight, strength, and courage.

It is important that they rely on her and consult her concerning the advice they should give in directing individuals in the spiritual life, especially those who seem destined to attain a high degree of perfection and a particularly great apostolic influence.

Hence, it is Jesus that Mary wants priests to configurate in souls. They should present Jesus as the ideal to be followed. It is for Jesus that souls should be enthusiastic and not for some practice or virtue. Practices and virtues should never be seen other than as means to facilitate living the very life of Jesus. Perfection consists in imitating Jesus as closely as possible. *For those whom he foreknew he also predestined to be conformed to the image of his*

Son, in order that he might be the first-born among many brethren (Rom 8:29).

Spiritual direction can be given in a variety of ways. It can be given during the sacrament of reconciliation, by scheduled appointments, or by correspondence, in lectures to special groups, through conferences, etc. Every individual has particular needs and gifts. To guide a person into total resemblance to Jesus, spiritual direction should be in harmony with these needs and gifts. All the same, there are salient traits of the divine model that are appropriate for everyone. They are the three great loves of Jesus.

First of all, there is His love for the Father. It was this love that moved Him to come to earth in order to offer His Father a worthy sacrifice. It induced Him to accept a multitude of tasks, to submit to numerous humiliations, to drink the chalice from which His human nature recoiled, to shed His Blood and to give up His life. The priest should urge the one coming to him for guidance to imitate this filial love of Jesus and help him understand that the Father of Jesus is his infinitely loving Father also, and that as his son he should love him in return and abandon himself to him. By remaining close to Jesus, his Brother, and to Mary, his Mother, he will instinctively take on this filial attitude toward the Father.

Secondly, there is His love for His Mother. Next to His Father, it was Mary that Christ loved most of all, more than all other creatures together. The priest should lead his protégé to imitate the filial piety of Jesus towards His Mother. A true and perfect devotion to Mary consists in this imitation and not in emotional feelings, in formulas of prayer, or in devotional practices. As it was for Jesus, it is belonging entirely to Mary, loving her, honoring her, obeying her, praising her, and working with her and for her.[36] The spiritual director who leads an individual to Christ through Mary finds his work greatly simplified. As long as this individual's devotion to Mary is only a superficial one, he runs into many obstacles, has need of much counseling and only imperfectly understands the advice given him. Once he has a proper understanding of Mary, his life is marvelously simplified. On his own, he finds solutions to difficulties that once confounded him. On his own, he sees the resolutions he should make. His spiritual director merely has to approve what he proposes and, from time to time, call his attention to some particular point.

---

36 Cf. E. Neubert, My Ideal, Jesus, Son of Mary.

Thirdly, there is Christ's love for all men and women. The Word was made flesh to save them, to save His Mother, first of all, in an exceptional way, and then, with her, to save all others. A person is not imitating Christ, in fact is not a Christian, if he is not concerned for the salvation of his brothers and sisters. The great commandment for all Christians is to love others as Christ loved them, and He loved them to the point of giving up His life to save them. Again, it is through Mary that a spiritual director can effectively inculcate a true missionary spirit into the one he is guiding. It is by explaining the apostolic mission of the Blessed Virgin in the world, the consequence of her mission as mother, as Coredemptrix, as Distributrix of all graces.[37] It is by showing him that, in this era, every effective and lasting apostolate is one undertaken in the name of Mary (Marian Sodalities, Legion of Mary, Militia of the Immaculate, Actio Mariana, the Marian retreats given by the Pallotine Fathers, Lourdes, Fatima, Marian pilgrimages, etc.). This is a good time to be alive; it is the age of Mary.

Women comprise the greater number of those who ask a priest for spiritual direction. It is important in these instances to exercise a good

---

37 Cf. E. Neubert, My Ideal, Jesus, Son of Mary, chapters 1 through 4.

deal of tact. Some priests are puritanical and rigid in their dealings with women. Other priests belittle them, provoking their disgust. Still others are overly familiar with them, possibly endangering themselves or the women. In any case, they risk giving scandal and are unable to render any spiritual assistance. History and daily experience demonstrate that women are capable of attaining a high degree of perfection and of exercising a widespread apostolic influence. If the faith and religious practice are vibrant in certain places, in spite of a clergy tainted by secularist or Jansenistic ideas, it is the women— mothers of families and religious educators—who are responsible.

If a priest lives in close union with his heavenly Mother, the ideal Woman, he will not be rigid or scornful or overly familiar with any women he has contact with in his ministry. He will see in them sisters of Mary, the Virgin, the Spouse, the Mother. He will interact with them, as with Mary herself, and he will always seek Mary's help in the guidance he gives them. He will lead them to a true devotion to Mary—not emotional or sentimental, but solid—as is that of filial piety towards Jesus. It should be an imitation of their Mother, offering themselves and suffering as she did for Jesus and the salvation of souls.

Women have a reputation for being complicated, preoccupied with how they look and how others see them. Yet, there are many women who are forthright and candid, women who have learned from Mary how to be unselfish and totally dedicated to Jesus and His interests. They are capable of attaining a high degree of union with Christ as well as impressive apostolic successes. May their spiritual directors help them become more and more like Mary, and auxiliaries in the priestly ministry as she is.

CHAPTER TWENTY-EIGHT

Preaching an Authentic Christ with Mary

The Son of God came into this world *to bear witness to the truth* (Jn 18:37). During His public life, He preached throughout the land, morning, noon, and night, without ceasing. He preached in marketplaces and open fields, on mountains and in desert places, and even from a boat on the seaside. It was because He gave testimony to the Truth that He was tried, condemned, and put to death. Before leaving His apostles to go to His Father,

He commanded them, *Go and make disciples of all nations…teaching them to observe all that I have commanded you* (Mt 28:19–20).

The apostles understood. As soon as the Holy Spirit descended upon them, Peter began preaching to the Jews and, in response to his first sermon, three thousand were converted. In order to give themselves more fully *to prayer and the ministry of the word* (Acts 6:4), the Twelve appointed deacons to attend to material affairs. Within a short time, they were scattered through the world preaching Jesus Christ and converting persons of good will in all the nations.

No one preached more than St. Paul and no one brought more disciples to Christ than he. *I preach the gospel*, he said, … *for necessity is laid upon me. Woe to me if I do not preach the gospel!* (1 Cor. 9:16). And he explains the reason for this necessity: *For, 'every one who calls upon the name of the Lord will be saved.' But how are men to call upon him in whom they have not believed? And how are they to believe in him of whom they have never heard? And how are they to hear without a preacher?* (Rom 10:13–14). At the present time, more than two thirds of humanity have not heard of Christ, and of those who have, how many have been told of His life and teaching?

It is for the priest, he who stands in the place of Christ and the apostles, to preach Christ, making Him better known to those who know Him already, and revealing Him to those who do not yet know Him or know little of Him. It is for the priest to evangelize not only from the pulpit and in the classroom, but also in lectures, public discussions, and private conversations. Priests must proclaim Christ by spoken word and in written word (books, magazines, newspapers, pamphlets), each one according to his gifts and his grace.

It was not Mary's mission to preach, but it was her mission to give Christ to the world. In making Christ known to men and women, then, the priest is helping Mary in her mission. How ardently she desires success in his preaching. The content of this preaching, as it is understood here, is not an explanation of morality or the Commandments, but the Gospel, which is the teaching of Christ, or better yet, the person of Christ.

The crowds, though ignorant of His Divinity, were enthralled by the person of Christ. They were irresistibly captivated by His charm and could listen to Him for an entire day. Wherever He spoke they came, following Him into desert places, forgetful of their concerns and even their hunger. During the first three centuries of our era, it was the person of

Christ that enabled men, women, and children of all nations—civilized and uncivilized people who had only recently renounced their pagan vices and errors—to joyfully shed their blood in witnessing to Him. And it is still true that any priest who has meditated on Christ at great length and lovingly absorbed His spirit, arouses the same enthusiasm and dedication today, when preaching to an assembly. No one knows the inner life of Christ as Mary does, and no one is a better tutor for making it known to a priest than Mary.[38]

A priest must preach the teaching of Christ, the unvarnished Gospel, including all its requirements. Above all, he must preach charity, the new commandment of the Master, His distinctive commandment. Not a theatrical charity that consists of almsgiving and ingratiating behavior, but a charity that forgives sincerely, that prays for calumniators and persecutors, and that returns good for evil. It is a charity that not only donates, but donates self without counting the cost or the sacrifice; a charity which, when circumstances call for it, gives one's life for others. Christ did all this and expected His disciples to follow the example He has given. Who understood and practiced *this* charity better than the Virgin of Nazareth, the Virgin of Calvary? Anyone

---

38 Pope Saint Pius X, Ad diem illum, n.7.

who lives in close union with her cannot help but take on her charity.

A priest must preach total self-abnegation. He must make it clear to those who are concerned only for their own personal well-being and pleasure that, if they are not ready to deny themselves and carry the cross each day, they are not truly disciples of Christ, even if they donate huge sums to the Church and its works. They may claim His name but they are not really His. When one is in the company of the Mother of Sorrows, this difficult lesson, this lesson of love, is instinctively understood.

A priest must preach Christ's teaching concerning earthly goods. It is not only to the poor and for their acceptance of their unhappy status that he quotes the words of Jesus, *Blessed are you poor* (Lk 6:20), … *Woe to you who are rich... It is easier for a camel to go through the eye of a needle than for a rich man to enter the kingdom of God* (Mt 19:24). Jesus addressed these words to the rich and it is the wealthy that the priest must warn about the danger of suffering the lot of the greedy rich. It is to the wealthy that he must preach the social teachings of the Church and explain that if they ignore it, they will find themselves among those to whom Christ said, *Woe to you that are rich, for you have received your consolation. Woe to you that are full now, for you shall hunger. Woe to you that laugh now, for you shall mourn and weep* (Lk 6:24–25; Mt 19:24). It is only the priest who has meditated with Mary on the poverty of Christ, and who has an understanding and love for priestly poverty, who has the power and the courage to bring these austere teachings to the attention of the rich.

A priest must preach the need of sacrificing everything rather than risk one's eternal salvation. *It is better to enter life maimed or lame than with two hands or two feet to be thrown into the eternal fire* (cf. Mt 18:8). It is He, the one who sacrificed His entire life to save us from damnation, who has the authority to give these admonitions.

Anyone who preaches an edited gospel, a gospel adapted so as not to offend the rich or the squeamish, betrays Christ. Priests who have fearlessly preached the authentic Christ, with all His clemency and all His demands, are not those who have sought applause, but who have disturbed the complaisant and won over the disposed. A priest who speaks in his own name, however intelligent and eloquent he may be, speaks as a man.

People applaud and then forget. A priest who quotes the Gospel with all its lessons of love and renouncement speaks in the name of God. He is courageous because he feels strong with the power of the Master whose instrument he is. The power to be demanding does not come from him.

He knows that it is Christ Himself who is demanding. And it is to this Christ—who practiced all that He taught and much more, whose very demands express love—that one surrenders. This is the Christ Mary knew and the one she reveals to those who meditate on Him with her. She will obtain for them the special gift of preaching Him and, in their preaching, the ability to enlighten, to convince, to influence, to transform.

CHAPTER TWENTY-NINE

With Mary, Preaching Jesus by Example

Priests should preach Jesus by their conduct more than by their words. It was the person of Jesus, more than His preaching, that won Him disciples ready to accept His teaching and to die with Him. The history of the Church bears out the fact that throngs of people were converted by observing the abnegation and charity marking the lives of the first Christians, or by merely taking notice of the example of St. Anthony or St. Francis of Assisi or many others who never preached. Daily experience shows that a simple word authenticated by a holy life is much more efficacious than exhortations which are most eloquent but not coupled with a Christ-like life.

The preaching of a priest is heard only from time to time. His example is a continuous sermon about Jesus. When is this so? It is when it exemplifies the behavior of Christ. If he unfailingly acts as another Christ, he continually makes Jesus known and loved and served.

Priestly composure indicates an interior union with Jesus, if and when he carries out his duties in Christ's name. This composure is a manifestation of priestly dignity. Some priests seem to think that priestly dignity requires them to be stern and aloof. Others believe that in order to be all things to all men they should ignore their priestly distinction and be a good buddy to everyone. No one ever comported themselves with greater dignity than Jesus and Mary and yet no one was less rigid, less prim, or less aloof than They. If a priest notes their conduct carefully he will know how priestly dignity requires him to act.

On one occasion, the Pharisees made this declaration to Jesus, *Teacher, we know that you speak and teach rightly, and show no partiality, but truly teach the way of God* (Lk 20:21). Would that every priest merited that acknowledgement. Would that there never be any insincerity, any twisting of the truth, any subterfuge, any trickery in speech or action in any priest. At times some sophistry might be of help to a confessor in showing mercy to a sinner, but it should never be found in his normal interaction with others. Let his speech be *Yes or No* (Mt 5:37), and he will always have people's confidence. A priest's teaching should always be genuine. If he does not practice what he preaches, he is no better than the Pharisees, and he deserves the imprecations Christ pronounced against them.

Christ was poor and He took delight in their company. Priests should have a similar attitude. They should love the impoverished with His love and treat them with respect, not condescendingly. As clergymen, they give special honor to those citizens of heaven the pope has declared "Blessed." Let them give special honor to the citizens of earth that Christ has declared "Blessed." As for the rich, they should be respectfully made aware of the obligations their wealth imposes on them, and the dangers to which it exposes them.

Christ was never self-serving. Everything He did was for the good of His Father and the benefit of souls. The priest who is suspected of always looking out for his personal interests—money, narcissism, ambition—has little influence on others. On the other hand, people feel attracted to the priest who is oblivious of himself, who seeks only to be of help to others, who gives equal service to all. And if his devotion goes to the point of constant, total self-sacrifice, they are unfailingly won over by his charity and willingly follow his guidance.

To sum it all up, the priest who resembles Jesus is the priest who can preach with success. It is the role of Mary to fashion his resemblance to Jesus. For the power of winningly preaching Christ to people, it suffices to allow oneself to be formed by Mary, to become more and more like her Son.

Isn't this the reason—aside from the work of grace—that explains the great ministerial effectiveness of Mary's devotees? Their constant union with her led them to absorb her spirit, which is none other than the spirit of Jesus. It is this spirit of Jesus that people recognize in them and that wins them over to Christ's cause.

CHAPTER THIRTY

The Responsibility of Making Mary Known

It is not enough to encourage the faithful to have devotion to Mary. They must be given sound Marian doctrine to nourish this devotion. A purely sentimental devotion melts away like the emotion that prompted it. Sentiment vacillates; doctrine endures. True devotion is based on doctrine.

Our Lord declared, *The words that I have spoken to you are spirit and life* (Jn 6:63). Everything else being equal, the more sound the doctrine, the more ardent and fruitful the devotion. These principles are valid for every time and place. But a solid devotion based on the truths of the Faith must especially be preached today.

The faithful are surrounded by unbelievers and token Christians who joke about displays of Marian piety and try to belittle Marian devotion. The life or death battle that modern day atheism is waging against the idea of God and anything supernatural, makes it vitally important that the Christians of today possess a sound and life-giving faith that protects them from the germs of spiritual death. A well-founded devotion to Mary innately creates such an atmosphere. This insight was echoed in a lecture given by Cardinal J. MacGuignan, the Archbishop of Toronto, at the closing of the International Marian Congress in Rome (1950) on the eve of the dogmatic definition of the Assumption. "It is the Marian heart of the Catholic faithful, a monument more enduring than perennial bronze that the Church expects us to nurture. One of the present-day, primary concerns of Pope Pius XII was the plight of a major part of the world's faithful who are strongly tempted, by deception and falsehood, to abandon Christ. For the protection of the people of God, nothing is more efficacious than true Marian devotion. That is the undeniable lesson of history and revealed truth."

Then the Cardinal challenged the Marian devotees he faced: "I wish to emphasize as strongly as I can that an easily understood Mariology be published as soon as possible. I mean a Mariology that is simple, clear and appealing—deeply theological but without speculative nuances— adapted to the educational levels and to the needs of all social classes and available in every language."[39]

---

[39] Cf. Alma Socia Christi, Acta Congressus Mariologici, Roma, 1950, Vol. 1, p. 241.

Unfortunately there are some Catholic factions directed by priests who, under the pretext of safeguarding the priority of devotion to Christ, minimize as much as possible devotion to Mary. No doubt these new-model apostles have not read nor understood what Pope Saint Pius X had already written in his encyclical, *Ad diem illum,* in 1904: "Mary is a sure and most efficacious assistance for us to arrive at the knowledge and love of Jesus Christ. Those, alas, seduced by the wiles of the demon or deceived by false doctrines furnish us with a peremptory proof of it by their conduct, thinking they can do without the help of the Virgin. Hapless are they who neglect Mary under pretext of the honor to be paid to Jesus Christ! As if the Child could be found elsewhere than with the Mother!"[40]

On the other hand, there is striking evidence that—by the Will of God, of Mary, and of the Holy See as well, and by an instinctive drive of the Catholic faithful—our contemporary years are a Marian age *par excellence.*

And yet, in order for this age to become all that God wills it to be, and so that the renewal of the world through Mary's intervention can be fully achieved, it is necessary that every Catholic

---

40 Pope St. Pius X, Ad diem illum, n.15.

be completely informed about the place God has assigned to the Blessed Virgin in the work of human salvation.

What should priests teach about the Blessed Virgin? Evidently, sound doctrine and well-founded facts! The eminence of Mary is beyond anything we can imagine and the authentic evidence of her love for us is so clear that there is no need to propound questionable explications. On the other hand, while they should promote her honor with what is certain or very probable, they should not detect exaggerations and legends everywhere and feel called upon to quash them. Ordinary people sometimes express their very orthodox faith in inexact terms. When the occasion arises, their terminology can be ameliorated without labeling it heresy. They do give credence to some legends, but before setting out to discredit these stories, priests should ask themselves whether such rectification would not destroy their devotion as well. Knowingly teaching a legend as a fact is a lie; but clinging to a legend is not a sin against the Faith.

It would be well to ponder the advice St. Paul gave some Christians in Rome who, aware that nothing is evil in itself, ate meat that had been sacrificed to idols, thereby giving scandal to some of their less informed fellow religionists. *Do not let what you eat cause the ruin of one for whom Christ died* (Rom 14:15). There are priests full of book knowledge who, by their smirk, demeanor, remarks, or critiques do much harm to the unsophisticated faithful, or at least aggrieve their most sacred sensibilities.

The field of Marian doctrine is immense. Priests should teach each of the faithful what is appropriate to his frame of mind, education, and needs. However, it seems advisable to give a basic education to everyone on three particular points: the life of Mary, her privileges, and devotions to her.

The life of Mary is presented by explaining the scriptural passages that mention her.

Her privileges should be listed and the significance of each of them should be explained as precisely as possible, according to the character of one's audience. The grounds for them should be pointed out; their relations to each other should be spelled out and their consequences set forth. More than the nature of these privileges, it is what they reveal about her role that should be emphasized. Her divine Maternity, obviously, but also her spiritual Maternity, her roles as Coredemptrix and

Distributrix of graces, and her apostolic mission, especially at the present time, should be described.

These roles shed light on our relations with the Blessed Virgin and bring them down to earth.

As for devotion to Mary, its importance, its basis, and its goal—which is above all to promote living the life of Jesus—should be covered. Devotion to her should be stressed as Christocentric, especially by presenting it as the imitation of Christ's filial piety towards his Mother.[41]

Instructions about Mary should be given with conviction and love. Marian doctrine needs to be understood but, even more, it needs to be cherished.

More than the priest's knowledge about Mary, it is his tone of conviction and his enthusiastic bearing that will embed this feeling about Mary in the hearts of his listeners. If, before speaking about the Mother of Jesus, he asks her Son to make him worthy and

---

41 Father Neubert wrote several books treating these three points in which he pointed out what every priest, religious, adult Catholic, and Catholic child should know about the Blessed Virgin. They are: Vie de Marie (Edit. Salvator, Mulhouse), Marie dans le Dogme (Edit. Spes, Paris), La Devotion a Marie (Edit. Mappus, LePuy), Notre Mere, Pour la mieux connaitre (Edit, Mappus), and Votre Maman du Ciel (Edit. Mappus).

capable of sounding her praises and of making her loved and served, he can be sure of success and he will do more for promoting Christian life than any eloquent sermon would do.

CHAPTER THIRTY-ONE

Victim with the Christ-Priest with the Aid of Mary

Christ is both Priest and Victim. Since they share in His priesthood, priests ought also to share in Christ's status as victim. The Sacrifice of the Mass and the prayers offered in the name of the Church during Liturgy have the same value, no matter who the celebrant is. However, since the efficacy of these prayers varies according to the devotion of the priest, those of a priest who is holy and who is victim as well as priest, are more beneficial than those offered by a mediocre priest.[42] What member of the faithful, who wants to have a Mass celebrated for a special intention, would not feel more confident

---

[42] Thomas Aquinas, *Summa Theologicae*, III, q.82, a.6, c.

of a positive response if the celebrant should be the Cure of Ars rather than a worldly priest? Moreover, priests are continuously priests. They are not priests only when they celebrate Mass. They are continuously about the business of glorifying God and saving souls, and they do this to the extent that they resemble Christ as victim.

Our Lord expects more of a priest than mere material cooperation. In sharing His priesthood with men, He desires a *human* collaboration, one that is knowing and free. He wants a man who understands His dispositions and makes them his own. Every priest ought to claim as his own St. Paul's words to the Colossians, *I rejoice in my sufferings for your sake, and in my flesh I complete what is lacking in Christ's afflictions for the sake of his body, that is, the Church* (Col 1:24). The Apostle does not say that he suffers simply to show Christ his love or to add his sufferings to those of Christ, but to complete *what is lacking* in the sufferings of Christ. What a strange claim! Doesn't the Passion of Christ have an infinite value? In itself, yes; in its application, no. Pope Pius XII, in his encyclical on the Mystical Body of Christ states, "Although our Savior's cruel passion and death merited for his Church an infinite treasure of graces, God's inscrutable providence has decreed that these graces should not be granted to us all at once, but their greater or lesser abundance will depend in no small part on our own good works, which draw down on the souls of men a rain of heavenly gifts freely bestowed by God."[43] All the members of the Mystical Body are closely united to each other but, by his calling, the priest has a greater responsibility than the laity in the application of the merits of the Passion to his brothers and sisters.

This truth is difficult to accept for many priests. They want to celebrate Mass, administer the sacraments, preach, teach catechism, and even offer many extra prayers for their charges. Having done all this, they consider themselves to be good priests. Good priests? Are they perpetuating the one and only Priest, the crucified Christ? Every great apostle embraced the cross. The saintly Abbe Poppe said, "Working is good; praying is better; suffering is best of all." He also said. "Souls are saved to the extent that one suffers for them." It was by means of his sufferings that the Cure of Ars transformed his parishioners from backsliders into practitioners as fervent as the first Christians. He asked his neighboring fellow priests—who claimed their situation was beyond recovery, that they had done all that they could, and to no avail—whether

---

43 Pope Piux XII, The Mystical Body of Christ, n.107.

they had fasted, used the discipline on themselves, or slept on the bare floor. Christ Himself said that there are evil spirits that only prayer and fasting can drive out (cf. Mt 17:19; Mk 9:28). And was it not by the Cross that He saved us?

Many souls are lost because many of Christ's ordained are unwilling to be both priest and victim. No doubt these "good priests" save many souls, but do they save a third or even a sixth of those they could save were they to immolate themselves, in addition to giving absolutions and offering prayers?

I am unwilling to suffer. I decline to save all the souls I could save. I avoid the opportunity to change eternal curses into eternal songs of love. I see hundreds, maybe thousands, of souls that God wishes me to minister to as a priest. Will they be lost, hating God and hating me for all eternity? Or will they be cherished children of my Father and my heavenly Mother, blessing Them and blessing me forever with all their hearts? Yes or no? It all depends on whether I refuse or accept to suffer for them.

How is it possible for a priest to live out this total self-immolation that so terrifies weak human nature, not in the future he envisioned on his ordination day, but in the disheartening reality of everyday and every hour? Again, it is by frequent meditation on Christ, Priest and Victim, a personal, loving meditation made in union with the Sorrowful Mother. He will show the way, and she will explain it and enable the priest to follow it lovingly and generously. Review His life from its initial moment when He offered Himself to the Father in place of the sacrifices of the Old Law, through His Hidden and Public Life, and through His Passion to His final words, *It is finished* (Jn 19:30). He never wavered from that first self-offering; He renewed it at every step of His life.

It was a truly *total* sacrifice that He continuously suffered. He sacrificed Himself as completely as possible with all the excruciating intensity that would come to a perfect humanity united to the Divinity. His physical sensitivity was greater than any other, a sensitivity He refused to lessen when he abstained from the dulling potion offered him. It was a sensitivity endured to its extreme limit to the point of needing help with His Cross on the way to Calvary, and expiring more quickly than was ordinarily the case in crucifixions.

But it was especially in His soul that Christ suffered, because He suffered to the extent that He loved, beyond all human comprehension. During His Hidden Life, He suffered because of the sins of the chosen people and because He was always aware of Simeon's prophecy concerning His Mother there beside Him. During His Public Life, He suffered because of the people's failure to understand and the hardheadedness of His apostles as well, and because of the bad faith, hypocrisy, hate, and lies of His enemies. He suffered above all during His Passion, knowing that He had taken upon Himself all the sins of the world, even those most despicable and repugnant. The sins of chosen souls and the ruin of a great number of souls—especially those of priests—were particularly wounding to Him. Is it any surprise, then, that during the agony, revulsion, and terror He underwent in the Garden of Olives, He asked that this chalice be withdrawn from Him? Yet, He agreed to drink it because it was an essential part of His priesthood, a priesthood of love. It is this love of Christ for souls that priests should ponder, standing beside His Mother, attempting, with her help, to enter the core of His divine Heart.

It is possible for a priest to penetrate His Heart even more deeply if he also enters the Sorrowful and Immaculate Heart of Mary. From the moment of her Immaculate Conception, her response to God, who gave her existence in this pure state, was the total gift of herself to the Creator for whatever he should ask of her. At the moment of the Incarnation, this gift became priestly. She knew the doleful mission of the Messiah from having read of the Prophet Isaiah. She understood that in becoming the Mother of the Man of Sorrows, she would become the Mother of Sorrow. Her response was simply, *Behold the handmaid of the Lord, let it be done to me according to your word* (Lk 1: 38). From then on, her life was one of indescribable suffering because of her union with the Christ-Priest. Apart from Jesus, she might enjoy a serene existence, but she would have no existence apart from Jesus. The sufferings occasioned by her Maternity included the refusal of the citizens of Bethlehem to receive her at the time of Jesus' birth, the prophecy of Simeon, the flight into Egypt, the disappearance of Jesus. Then there was the news she received that the Pharisees and the priests threatened Him by their lies and their determination to be rid of Him. Most of all, there was the sight of the tortures inflicted on the Body of her Son and the indescribable agony in Jesus' soul, an agony she felt within her own soul. Jesus was the cause of them all. She suffered to the extent that she loved because these sufferings were caused by her love. The depth of her love was more than we can imagine, and so is the intensity of her martyrdom.

She embraced all these sufferings with her whole heart, and in no way would she seek to lessen them because she suffered for Jesus, with Jesus, and for the same intentions of Jesus—for the glory of the Father and the salvation of all men and women, her children.

O Christ, You loved me and You offered Yourself for me! O Mary, you loved me and offered yourself for me! Help me to love you and to offer myself for you and with you, for the Father and for souls!

> *O thou Mother! fount of love!*
> *Touch my spirit from above.*
> *Make my heart with thine accord.*
> *Make me feel as thou hast felt;*
> *Make my soul to glow and melt*
> *With love of Christ our Lord.*

What are the sacrifices that mark the life of a victim? In most cases, they are not those practiced by the Cure of Ars. Immolations of that kind need a special sign from God. It is not necessary that those around a priest be aware of his self-sacrifice. But it is necessary that they never see him dissipated. Priestly self-sacrifice takes on all sorts of forms according to the individual and the circumstances. The priest who has the spirit of a victim will be ingenious in discovering suitable practices. It is sufficient here to offer a few general guidelines.

1. In the matter of food, drink, clothing, and lodging, follow the advice St. Paul gave to Timothy.

If we have food and clothing, with these we shall be content (1 Tim 6:8). Give bodily needs all the care necessary for remaining fit to carry out the service of God and souls, but nothing more than that.

2. Carry out all the sacrifices associated with the practice of priestly virtues (charity, humility, chastity, obedience, modesty, etc.) but without seeking compensation. Human nature is ingenious in finding some counterbalance for the sacrifices grace inspires. Be on guard! All that God wants without seeking reward!

3. Accept the anguish God sends or permits (heat, cold, fatigue, enfeeblement, sickness). Accept the trials that come in associating with others: lack of respect, impoliteness, rudeness, nasty moods, eccentricities, misunderstandings and even those worse trials which will be treated in the next chapter. Accept all this with a good heart, without complaining, without speaking of them unless some responsibility obliges it. Submitting to them with a sullen attitude is a failure to recognize them as gifts Jesus sent out of love and as ways to help Him. Let them bring a smile; it is a smile at Jesus. Conversing about them without necessity is a way of seeking compensation and a way of losing nine tenths of their spiritual value. They are for Jesus' ears only, helping Him save souls. Don't just tolerate them;

one does not tolerate a gift. Embrace them and say "Thank You" to Jesus and Mary.

4. Offer all sufferings to Jesus and unite them to His. Sufferings in themselves have no value. They acquire value when they are united to Christ's sufferings. He it is that spiritualizes them and confers on them the efficacy of His Passion. To make this offering with complete sincerity and total love, present them in the hands of Mary.

5. Add to these unavoidable trials some voluntary mortifications. Unsought trials are abundant, and they are the most efficacious of sufferings if they are accepted with love and thanksgiving. However, voluntary mortifications are also necessary as a way of maintaining a spirit of self-sacrifice and a readiness to accept unavoidable trials with a proper attitude. At times, they can help in obtaining a difficult favor or in expiating a particular sin.

Should we ask God to send us trials? If we do, are we sure this is the will of God? Are we sure we will have the strength to endure them? What we can do is ask the Blessed Mother to send us those trials she wishes us to face, along with the power to undergo them, as she desires.

CHAPTER THIRTY-TWO

Undergoing Priestly Trials and Crises with Mary

Many priests encounter trials and even crises in their lives. They sometimes have very unhappy endings. Do priests living in close union with Mary escape them?

Priestly crises, properly understood, are spiritually troubling states of the soul which, at times, present a real danger of infidelity to the priestly vocation or to the Christian faith. At other times, it can lead to a withering of initial ideals of holiness and zeal, in favor of a mediocre or even sinful existence.

The major priestly crises have to do with sexuality, obedience, ambition, and the Faith.

Priests very devoted to Mary, no doubt encounter temptations in all of these areas. Their closeness to her does not eliminate the consequences of original sin. But for them, these temptations do not lead to full-force crises or even occasional, grave failures, as long as their closeness to her is intact. When these temptations are especially strong, they meditate again on the manner in which the Blessed Virgin is forming them.[44]

However, crises of faith can occur among priests very dedicated to Mary as a result of their studies, the influence of colleagues, or the impact of new ideas that surface in times of religious or social turmoil. Such was the case during the modernism period. Yet, it must be observed that at such difficult times, priests deeply dedicated to Mary, who were strongly pressured by the theories and popularity of these new mentors, remained faithful to the Church. Some other priests, who lacked a close union with Mary, foundered. Marian devotees are bound to a supernatural power that holds them fast, even when their minds are in ferment.[45]

There are other trials that fall upon priests devoted to the Blessed Virgin. Every trial is a cross and every cross includes a grace. Mary is the Distributrix of all graces. She is there for these priests, generally speaking, not to alleviate the trial, but always to help them acquire the grace it holds.

---

44 Cf. the matching chapters in Part Two.
45 The denial of Mary's virginity by some innovators opened the eyes of many priests and kept them true to the traditional faith.

There are bodily trials: infirmities, sicknesses, impoverishment, enfeeblement that necessitate inaction. Mary will teach the priest by her example how—without preaching, administering the sacraments, or leaving his seclusion—he can help the Christ-Priest glorify God and save souls. There are also those disconcerting trials which anger or discourage any priest who sees things only from a human point of view: mockery, reprimands, stumbling blocks placed by worldly laity or tepid confreres, and ridicule or jealousy. To these, one can add apathy, misunderstandings, disapprovals, and opposition from those who should encourage or help him. Together with the Blessed Virgin, the priest undergoing such trials will meditate on Christ opposed, mocked, calumniated, and condemned to death by those who should have supported and assisted him.

There are still worse trials. A priest disregards the obstacles and goes all out to succeed. Yet, his efforts end in a checkmate. How devastating, if he has to admit he failed because of his eccentricities, his ignorance, his blunder, or his slip-up! At Mary's side, he will regain his peace of mind. With her, he will ask himself whether he was depending on himself or on Jesus and his Mother. If on himself, he will accept the failure as expiation and a lesson for the future. He will ask the Blessed Virgin to accept his humiliation as a sacrifice on behalf of the souls he wishes to save. Saint Paul said, *We know that in everything God works for good* (Rom 8:28). And St. Augustine comments that this "everything" includes even our sins. The priest will also resolve to always work with her in the future. The harsher the lesson learned, the more gratifying the future will be.

If, on the other hand, the priest who failed really did act in the name of Christ and according to the intentions of Mary, let him meditate on Jesus and His Mother on Calvary. Let him admire once more the faith of Mary, in spite of the seeming failure of her Son's mission and the promises of Gabriel (cf. Lk 1:32–33). *Blessed is she who believed that there would be a fulfillment of what was spoken to her from the Lord* (cf. Lk 1:45). No one ended in greater disaster than the Crucified, and no one achieved a greater triumph than He! Whoever functions as Christ and Mary did, when he fails as They did, will triumph as They did!

Hail, O Cross, our only hope!

CHAPTER THIRTY-THREE

Priestly Joys and Mary

Priesthood does include the pursuit of joy; a priest is not a priest for his own benefit. But, without seeking it, a priest does experience great joy in the knowledge that he can give joy to Christ, to Mary, and to souls.

The priest gives joy to Christ. Jesus is happy to see in the priest a disciple who tries to imitate Him as closely as is possible for a simple human creature. He is especially happy because he does it with the help of Mary, allowing her to form him as completely as she can, into His own image, taking on His priestly virtues and dispositions. He sees in the priest, someone who associates Mary in his priesthood as He Himself did; one who does his best to reproduce His filial piety towards her and convince as many of the faithful as he can, to do the same. He sees in him, a disciple who effectively helps Him bring to the Father a large number of the men and women for whom He shed His Blood. Christ's happiness is the priest's happiness.

The priest gives joy to Mary. She is happy that this priest-son allows her to form him into the image of her First-born Son in order to become another Christ-Priest. She is happy to observe his filial dispositions towards her, recalling those Jesus had for her; and she is happy that, with his help, she can reclaim for God a host of sinners for whom she sacrificed her Son, making them other Christs. Mary's happiness is the priest's happiness.

The priest gives joy to souls. These are the souls—and who can count their number?—who would have been lost forever, had this priest not worked in close union with Mary. They now rejoice in the knowledge and love of the Father, the Son, the Holy Spirit, and their heavenly Mother. These are the souls who, without his help, would have remained mediocre Christians. He introduced them to a life of close union with Mary and they became generous apostles. The happiness of all these souls is the happiness of their priest.

Here on earth, all this happiness is mixed with much bitterness. But this does not bother the priest who has learned from Mary that this bitterness is actually a way of giving joy to Jesus, to Mary, and to souls. As did St. Paul, he can declare, *I am filled with comfort. With all our affliction, I am overjoyed* (2 Cor 7:4).

What will it be like when Mary's priest enters heaven to join those he was committed to love and serve on earth? What happiness will be his as he contemplates the Father whom he better understood, better loved, and better glorified because Mary helped him assimilate Jesus' filial piety towards the Father who will recognize in this priest, a son truly formed in the image of His First-Born, the Father to Whom he directed, thanks to Mary, so many of the faithful who, without his influence, might not have been counted among the blessed.

What happiness this priest will have when he meets the Christ-Priest whom he strove, under the direction of Mary, to imitate completely, who is grateful to him for having practiced and preached filial piety towards His Mother, and for having saved so many souls for whom, without his ministry, His Blood would have been shed in vain.

What happiness will be his as he meets the heavenly Mother he so often prayed to and loved; the one whose life, tenderness, power, and understanding he had preached of to the faithful so many times. She was the one who revealed Jesus to him and, little by little, transformed him to resemble Jesus. She it was who brought about the marvelous fruitfulness of his priesthood and who is now grateful to him for all he did to help her give glory to the Most Holy Trinity, to extend the Kingdom of her Son, and to bring eternal happiness to so many of her spiritual children saved by their joint efforts.

What joy will be his to see so many of the faithful—some whom he recognizes and some who are strangers—who come to thank him for all he did and suffered to bring about their salvation. And there will be others who do not owe their presence in heaven to him, but who see him as responsible for their degree of love and happiness, enabling them to give greater glory to the Holy Trinity and more joy to Christ, his Mother, and the other inhabitants of heaven—a love and happiness they would not have achieved had they remained in the mediocre state from which he reclaimed them in the name of Mary. And if he sincerely tried to be faithful to all his priestly and Marian graces while here on earth, then, as time continues to the very last day, he will see an increase in the population of the blessed in heaven and their capacity for happiness and giving glory, thanks to the influence his words and his life exercised, and continue to exercise on earth.

May the Father and the Son
and the Holy Spirit
be Glorified in All Places
Through the Immaculate

APPENDIX I

Prayers Expressing Total Consecration to Mary

-1-

O Mary, Mother of Jesus and my Mother, I give myself entirely to you, in order to imitate as perfectly as possible the filial love of Jesus for you and to battle under your orders for the conquest of souls.

-2-

Sovereign Mistress of heaven and earth, at the foot of your throne, where respect and love have enchained our hearts, we offer you our homage of service and praise, we consecrate ourselves to your worship and, with transports of joy, embrace a state of life where everything is done under your protection, and everyone pledges himself to praise you, to serve you, and to proclaim your greatness. Would that our zeal for the honor of your worship and the interests of your glory were able to make amends to you for all the assaults of heresy, the outrages of unbelief, and the indifference and neglect of the generality of mankind.

O Mother of our Redeemer! Dispenser of all graces! Extend the empire of religion in the souls of men; banish error, preserve and increase the Faith in this country; protect innocence and preserve it from the dangers of this world and from the allurements of sin. Aware of our necessities and favorable to our desires, obtain for us the charity which animates the just, the virtues which sanctify them, and the glory which is their crown. Amen.

-3-
Prayer of St. Anselm

O good Jesus, by the love with which You love Your Mother, grant, I beseech You, that I may truly love her as You loved her and desire her to be loved.

-4-
The Three O'clock Prayer

Lord Jesus, we gather in spirit at the foot of the Cross with Your Mother and the disciple whom You loved. We ask Your pardon for our sins, which are the cause of Your death. We thank You for remembering us in that hour of salvation and for giving us Mary as our Mother.

Holy Virgin, take us under your protection and open us to the action of the Holy Spirit.

St. John, obtain for us the grace of taking Mary into our lives as you did, and of assisting her in her mission.

-5-

O good Jesus, help us to love Mary, Your physical Mother and our spiritual Mother, as You loved her and wish her to be loved.

Mary, our Mother, help us to respond as faithful disciples to the call of Jesus. In the spirit of Blessed William Joseph Chaminade, help us to participate faithfully in your apostolic mission to present Jesus to the world about us, as you did and still do today.

We ask this grace in the name of Jesus, Son of Mary. May Jesus and Mary lead us into union with the Triune God. Amen.

-6-

We come, O holy Virgin, our good Mother, to offer you our sentiments of filial piety. To you, O holy Mary, my glorious Queen, to your blessed trust and special charge, and to the bosom of your mercy, this day and every day and at the hour of my death, I commend myself, my soul and my body. To you I commit all my hope and my consolation, my distresses and my miseries, my life and the end of my life that, by your most holy intercession and by your merits, all my actions may be directed and disposed according to your will and that of your Son. Amen.

-7-

O Mary, Virgin Immaculate, I firmly believe that the Son of God chose you to be His true Mother. I believe that, being your Son, He loved you and continues to love you more than all other creatures, and that He performed all the duties of a loving Son with infinite perfection.

I believe that He has deigned to associate you in His mission of redemption; that, in accordance with His will, no soul, guilty or innocent, will be sanctified and saved without your mediation; and that no one will come to Him except through you.

I believe that being His Mother, you are also mine. For, when you conceived Him at Nazareth, you conceived me; when you sacrificed Him on Calvary, you brought me forth to supernatural life; when you cooperate with Him in the distribution of all graces, you continue to nourish me and educate me as another Jesus.

I believe that He desires me to imitate His example and to strive as much as possible to be to you what He Himself always was and always will be.

Behold, I give and consecrate myself to you as your child, just as Jesus gave Himself to be your Son. I give you my body and my soul, whatever I have, am, do and can do. I give myself unreservedly and irrevocably, for time and for eternity. I give myself so that you may use me as you wish, demand of me any act of devotion, impose upon me any sacrifice—those that I foresee and those that are hidden from me, those that will be sweet and those at which nature will rebel. I fear nothing. I know to whom I am giving myself.

After the example of Jesus, I wish to love you with all the powers of my soul; I wish to honor, to obey, to imitate you; I wish to have full confidence in you, to be united constantly with you, and, in short, to reproduce with the utmost perfection all the dispositions of the filial love of your Divine Son, and to become under your tutelage, another Jesus in your regard.

I particularly wish to assist you in your providential mission. I wish to be your apostle and soldier in the warfare against Satan. I wish to combat in your name and to save your children from his grasp. I wish to fight for the glory of your name, to make you known, loved, and served. I am convinced that revealing you to men is the most effective way of revealing Jesus to them.

I am only a poor sinner—you know it well—full of defects, weaker and more inconstant than I can realize. But I put my confidence in you. I am not working in my own name. I shall be omnipotent because you are omnipotent with the Divine power of your Son, and because my interests are your interests, and my cause is your cause. I shall battle under your orders, confident that you will win the victory.

O Mary, Mother of Jesus and my Mother, for the glory of the Most Holy Trinity, for your honor and for the salvation of my soul and the souls of others, accept the offering I am making of myself to you and obtain for me the grace to be faithful to it to the end of my days. Amen.

APPENDIX II

About the Author

The author of this book, Fr. Emile Nicholas Neubert, was born in Ribeauvillé, France on May 8, 1878. In 1892 he entered the postulancy (minor seminary) of the Society of Mary (Marianists); he entered their novitiate in 1894, and made first profession of vows on Sept. 15, 1895. After further study and work as a teacher in schools of the Society, he made final profession of vows on Sept. 7, 1902. He was ordained a priest in Fribourg, Switzerland on Aug. 5, 1906, and was awarded the Doctorate in Theology from the University of Fribourg in 1907. His doctoral thesis, written under the direction of the well-known patrologist, J.-P. Kirsch, bore the title *Marie dans l'Eglise anténicéene* [Mary in the Pre-Nicean Church; no English translation available], was published in 1908. This study was the first doctoral thesis in patristics on the Mother of God ever to be presented in a Catholic faculty of theology. It initiated the career of one of the Mariologists most responsible for the development of this area of theology over the past century. Still more important to his career was the discovery, around this time, of the spiritual heritage of Bl.

William Joseph Chaminade, founder of the Society of Mary.

Between 1907 and 1921, Fr. Neubert labored in the United States for his Order—for the most part in Missouri and Ohio—serving as Master of Postulants and then of Novices. In 1921 he returned to Europe, taught philosophy briefly in Strasbourg and then, from 1922 through 1949, he acted as Rector of the Marianist Seminary in Fribourg. In 1935, he was one of the founding members of the prestigious Mariological Society of France, and a member of the International Marian Academy in Rome. The immense number of his books and articles, most of which enjoy broad appeal, are a testimony to the influence he exercised on the Marian movement of our times and the spirituality and apostolate associated with it. Among friends and correspondents who promoted his books are such great Marian figures as Mr. Frank Duff, founder of the Legion of Mary, and St. Maximilian M. Kolbe, founder of the Militia of the Immaculate and first City of the Immaculate [Niepokalanów] in Poland. Further bibliographical information can be found in the entry on him by his disciple, Fr. Théodore Koehler, in the *Dictionnaire de Spiritualité*, vol. 11, cc. 151–152 [English translation, Appendix

D of the *Autobiography of Father Emile Neubert, Marianist*, Dayton OH 2007, pp. 81–84].

Fr. Neubert died at Art-sur-Meurthe in France on August 29, 1967.

Fr. Neubert's contribution to Mariology and to Marian spirituality cannot be underestimated. His doctoral thesis is a milestone in the history of Mariology. It not only demonstrated the importance of Mary in the writings of the Fathers and how to go about a fruitful patristic study of her, but it also indicated the true place of Mary in the thought and life of the Church from its beginning. The soundness of this study, published at the height of the modernist controversy, was perhaps the most effective rejoinder to the then fashionable opinion of doctrinal historians, like J. Turmel, that Mary only came to occupy such a position long after Pentecost, with the insinuation that said position was an aberration.

More than this, however, he contributed immensely to the integration of Marian doctrine and Marian spirituality: the doctrine for the sake of Marian spirituality to become saints in and through Mary, and the spirituality grounded firmly in Marian doctrine. Two of his better known works: *Mary in Doctrine* (French edition 1933) and *Who is She?: The Life and Study of the Blessed Virgin* (French edition 1936), illustrate this very clearly. The second of these works inaugurated a series of studies intended to apply this spirituality to various states of life. *Mary in the Priestly Ministry* (2009 Academy of the Immaculate, New Bedford, MA [French original: *Marie et notre sacerdoce*]), is one of these. Others in the series dealt with religious life, Christian educators, the Christian family—all published in France after World War II.

According to Fr. Stanley, translator of *Mary in the Priestly Ministry* [cf. his memoir: *Our Lady's Dolphin*, in the *Autobiography* cited above, pp. 75–76], Father Neubert considered the following as his three most important works: *My Ideal, Jesus, Son of Mary* [French original published in 1933, a veritable best seller with over half a million copies sold in all languages and still in print]; *Mary in the Priestly Ministry* [French original published in 1952 and published for the first time in English (2009 Academy of the Immaculate, New Bedford, MA)]; and *The Life of Union With Mary* [French original published in 1954]. To the latter is closely related *The Soul of Jesus Contemplated in Union With Mary* [French original published in 1957]. Among Father Neubert's other available works in English are: *Living With Mary*; *Mariology of Fr. Chaminade*;

Marian Catholic Action; *Our Gift from God*; *Queen of Militants*. Those desirous to know more about this gifted priest may begin with the *Autobiography of Father Emile Neubert, Marianist*, cited above.

Fr. Neubert was a gifted scholar who devoted his entire life and all his energies to the service of God's Mother and ours. More than this, he was a holy priest and religious—totally consecrated to Mary—who lived the doctrine he proclaimed. The following passage from his *Autobiography* unintentionally confirms what so many who were blessed to enjoy his spiritual guidance realized: his humble, saintly love of the Blessed Virgin and all her children. Fr. Neubert recalls how an old friend from childhood days, after reading his *Life of Union with Mary*, remarked: "You have sucked devotion to Mary along with the milk of your mother." Fr. Neubert comments (p. xii):

> The reality, however, is altogether different. I did not start as a good and pious child. Only toward the end of my fifteenth year did devotion to Mary begin slowly to attract me. I never dreamed to become a Marian author, but thanks to providential circumstances, once I began writing articles and books on Marian themes, I widened my plans. I would include, if I lived long enough,

books on the Blessed Virgin that were proposed to me or that proposed themselves as I wrote. To sum up, my life did not unfold according to an internal logic, but according to another, superior logic. I thank Her who designed it. If my biography is to be written, I want it to be at the same time a book on the Blessed Virgin.

Fr. Peter Damian M. Fehlner, FI

A Selection of Books from the Academy of the Immaculate

A Month with Mary *Daily Meditations for a Profound Reform of the Heart in the School of Mary* *by Don Dolindo Ruotolo* This little book was written by a holy Italian priest Father Dolindo Ruotolo (1882–1970). Originally written as spiritual thoughts to his spiritual daughter, the work is comprised of thirty-one meditations for the month of May. The month of Mary is the month of *a profound reform of heart:* we must leave ourselves and adorn ourselves with every virtue and every spiritual good.

Jesus Our Eucharistic Love *by Fr. Stefano Manelli, FI* A treasure of Eucharistic devotional writings and examples from the saints showing their stirring Eucharistic love and devotion. A valuable aid for reading meditatively before the Blessed Sacrament.

Who is Mary? *Fr. Gabriele M. Pellettieri, FI* This book is a concise Marian catechism presented in a question/answer format. In this little work of love and scholarship the sweet mystery of Mary is unveiled in all its beauty and simplicity. It is a very helpful resource both for those who want to know the truth about Mary and those who want to instruct others.

Padre Pio of Pietrelcina *by Fr. Stefano Manelli, FI* This 144-page popular life of Padre Pio is packed with details about his life, spirituality, and charisms, by one who knew the Padre intimately. The author turned to Padre Pio for guidance in establishing a new Community, the Franciscans of the Immaculate.

Devotion to Our Lady *by Fr. Stefano M. Manelli, FI* This book is a must for all those who desire to know the beauty and value of Marian devotion and want to increase their fervent love towards their heavenly Mother. Since it draws abundantly from the examples and writings of the saints, it offers the devotee a very concrete and practical aid for living out a truly Marian life.

Do You Know Our Lady? *by Rev. Mother Francesca Perillo, FI* This handy treatise (125 pages) covers the many rich references to Mary, as prefigured in the Old Testament women and prophecies and as found in the New Testament from the Annunciation to Pentecost. Mary's role is seen ever beside her Divine Son, and the author shows how scripture supports Mary's role as Mediatrix of all Graces. Though scripture scholars can read it with profit, it is an easy read for everyone. Every Marian devotee should have a copy for quick reference.

Come Follow Me *by Fr. Stefano Manelli, FI* A book directed to any young person contemplating a religious vocation. Informative; with many inspiring illustrations and words from the lives and writings of the saints on the challenging vocation of total dedication in the following of Christ and His Immaculate Mother through the three vows of religion.

Saints and Marian Shrine Series
edited by Bro. Francis Mary, FI

Padre Pio – The Wonder Worker The latest on this popular saint of our times including inspirational homilies given by Pope John Paul II during the beatification and canonizarion celebrations in Rome. The first part of the book is a short biography. The second is on his spirituality, charisms, apostolate of the confessional, and his great works of charity.

A Handbook on Guadalupe This well-researched book on Guadalupe contains 40 topical chapters by leading experts on Guadalupe with new insights and the latest scientific findings. A number of chapters deal with Our Lady's role as the patroness of the pro-life movement. Well-illustrated.

Kolbe – Saint of the Immaculata Of all the books in the Marian Saints and Shrines series, this one is the most controversial and thus the most needed in order to do justice to the Saint, whom Pope John Paul II spoke of as "the Saint of our difficult century [twentieth]." Is it true, as reported in a PBS documentary, that the Saint was anti-Semitic? What is the reason behind misrepresenting this great modern day Saint? Is a famous Mariologist right in accusing the Saint of being in error by holding that Mary is the Mediatrix of all Graces? The book has over 35 chapters by over ten authors, giving an in-depth view of one of the greatest Marian saints of all times.

For a complete listing of books, tapes and CDs from the Academy of the Immaculate please refer to our catalog. Request a free catalog by email, letter, or phone via the contact information given below for the Academy of the Immaculate.

Special rates are available with 25% to 50% discount depending on the number of books, plus postage. For ordering books and further information on rates to book stores, schools and parishes: ***Academy of the Immaculate***, *124 North Forke Dr., Advance, NC 27006, Phone/FAX (888)90.MARIA [888.90.62742], E-mail academy@ marymediatrix.com.* Quotations on bulk rates by the box, shipped directly from the printery, contact: *Franciscans of the Immaculate, P.O. Box 3003, New Bedford, MA 02741, (508)996-8274, FAX (508)996-8296, E-mail: ffi@ marymediatrix.com. Website: www.marymediatrix.com.*